THE REGIMENTS

OF SCOTLAND

THE REGIMENTS
OF SCOTLAND

Their histories, badges, tartans, etc.

BY

J. B. KIRKWOOD, F.S.A.Scot.

THE MORAY PRESS
EDINBURGH
1949

ACKNOWLEDGMENTS

I SHOULD like to acknowledge the assistance which I have received in the writing of this book from a perusal of many regimental histories and other books too numerous to mention individually. I am indebted to the officers of the regimental depôts for their ready co-operation in supplying information about their respective regiments, to Colonel Alec Sprot, D.S.O., for many valuable suggestions and to Captain J. Telfer Dunbar, F.S.A.Scot. late Hon. Curator of the Scottish United Services Museum, Edinburgh Castle, for kindly revising the proofs. My thanks are also due to the various Commonwealth military authorities who have so courteously furnished particulars of Scottish units forming part of their defence forces.

The War Office have kindly supplied the list of Victoria Crosses won during the wars of 1914-18 and 1939-45.

Printed by C. J. COUSLAND AND SONS LTD., 30 Queen Street, Edinburgh
for THE MORAY PRESS, 57 George Street, Edinburgh
54 Bloomsbury Street, London, W.C.1.

CONTENTS

INTRODUCTION

It is a fitting tribute to the military ardour of the Scot that a Scottish regiment, The Royal Scots, should take pride of place as the oldest line regiment in the British Army.

The Royal Scots evolved from several bodies of Scottish troops which had been in the service of France and Sweden. After the French defeat at Agincourt in 1415 numbers of Scottish troops were sent to France in implement of the old alliance between Scotland and France and some of these troops were later formed into the Scottish Guard and the Scottish Men-at-Arms. In 1590 several companies of Scottish soldiers went to France to fight for Henry of Navarre and it was from what remained of these companies, augmented by some officers and men from the Guard and the Men-at-Arms, that the Royal Scots were formed in 1633. Two years later, there were absorbed into the regiment the remnants of thirteen Scottish regiments in the Swedish Army. Sir Walter Scott attributed the attraction of service in Continental armies to " the contempt of commerce entertained by young men having some pretence to gentility, the poverty of the country of Scotland and the national disposition to wandering and to adventure." Whatever the reasons that prompted so many young Scots to engage themselves as soldiers of fortune there is no doubt that they acquired a high military reputation throughout Europe and that they were specially distinguished for the valour and fidelity with which they performed their duty.

The other Lowland regiments, with the exception of the 2nd Battalion of The Cameronians (the old 90th Perthshire Light Infantry), were all raised before any of the Highland corps. The oldest of the Highland regiments, The Black Watch, was formed in 1739. The original idea of enrolling the disaffected Highland clans as soldiers of the British Army is generally ascribed to Lord-President Forbes of Culloden but it was Pitt (the Earl of Chatham) who persuaded the Government to put the scheme into effect. In his famous speech to

Parliament in 1766 Pitt had this to say of the Highland regiments :—" I sought for merit wherever it was to be found. It is my boast that I was the first Minister who looked for it and found it in the mountains of the north. I called it forth and drew into your service a hardy and intrepid race of men, who when left by your jealousy became a prey to the artifice of your enemies, and had gone nigh to have overturned the state in the war before the last. These men in the last war were brought to combat on your side ; they served with fidelity as they fought with valour, and conquered for you in every part of the world."

After the Rebellion of 1745 the wearing of Highland dress by any save Highland soldiers in the Government service was forbidden and between 1748 and 1757 (when two new Highland regiments were raised) the officers and men of The Black Watch were the only British subjects who could lawfully wear the kilt. In view of the picturesqueness of the kilt and its present day popularity as military dress it is strange to find that there was a time when the kilt was considered a deterrent to recruiting. In April 1809 an order was issued stating that as the population of the Highlands of Scotland was found to be insufficient to supply recruits for the whole of the Highland corps in His Majesty's Army, and as some of these corps, by laying aside their distinguishing dress, which was objectionable to the natives of South Britain, would induce the men of the English Militia to enter, the 72nd, 73rd, 74th, 75th, and 91st Regiments were ordered to discontinue wearing the Highland dress for the future. The scarcity of highlanders to fill the Highland regiments at this period can perhaps be accounted for by the fact that from 1740 to the end of that century no less than 50 Highland battalions had been raised. Even the playing of the bagpipes was at one time decreed a treasonable practice and it is recorded that one James Reid, a piper, was actually sentenced to death at York in November 1746. At his trial the Court held that a Highland regiment never marched without a piper and Reid's bagpipes were therefore in the eye of the law an instrument of war.

Up to 1881 the Lowland regiments were dressed like English line regiments although pipers had been given to some of them. The result was that they had to some extent lost their nationality and had as many English and Irish as Scots in their ranks. In 1881 the Lowland regiments, with the exception of the Scots Guards, were clothed in doublets and tartan trews and recovered much of their national character.

The general conditions of military service were for a long period very bad indeed. Towards the end of the 17th century the pay of the soldier was 8d. a day of which 6d. was set aside for his subsistence. From the remaining 2d. a day or £3, 0s. 10d. a year, 12/2d. per annum was deducted for the salary of the Paymaster-General and 8d. for Chelsea Hospital, leaving £2 8s. 0d. per annum which was made over to the commanding officer to pay for the soldier's clothing, including belt, bayonet and cartridge box. Even that meagre pay was always in arrear, often for years. Military discipline was rough and severe and recruiting was difficult. Commanding officers were given levy money for the purpose of keeping their units up to strength but this was never enough to cover the bounties that had to be paid and they were often glad to accept criminals from prison for whom they had to pay nothing.

The 19th century saw great changes. Terms of service remained normally for life up to 1847 but in that year first engagements were limited to 10 years with the Colours and an additional 12 years in the Reserve but men could take on up to 21 year.. Later under the " Short Service System " the period was still further reduced to 7 years with the Colours and 5 years with the Reserve. Pay was issued by the Paymaster and distributed by officers commanding companies who were held strictly accountable for it. Discipline gradually became more humane and in 1879 flogging was abolished. For some time previously the maximum number of strokes allowed had been reduced from a thousand to fifty. The increases in rates of pay and improvement in general conditions which have taken place in recent times reflect in some measure the changed attitude of the civil population towards the soldier following two world wars.

Under the army reorganisation scheme of 1881 the regimental numbers of the infantry were abolished and the line battalions were linked in pairs as territorial regiments. The Militia of each district was attached to the territorial regiment and later the Volunteer forces were included in the territorial system. In 1908 the Militia became Special Reserve battalions to train and provide drafts for the regular battalions in war, while the Volunteers and the Yeomanry were re-organised as the Territorial Force. In 1921 the Territorial Force was re-designated the Territorial Army and the Special Reserve ceased to exist. The Territorial Army is now in course of being re-organised following the 1939-45 war. The battalions of the Highland regiments, together with normal divisional units, will be grouped in the 51st Highland Division. One battalion of each of the Lowland regiments, with appropriate units of other arms, will be grouped in an Independent Infantry Brigade Group but it is understood that in the event of a future expansion of the Territorial Army in Scotland the next Infantry Division to be formed will be raised in the Lowlands and numbered the 52nd Lowland Division.

The Scottish regiments of the British Army included here are (1) the Cavalry, Guards and Infantry of the Line; and (2) the Yeomanry and Scouts, with, in addition, the three Anglo-Scot regiments, the London Scottish, Liverpool Scottish and Tyneside Scottish. The twelve regiments forming the first category comprise one Cavalry regiment, The Royal Scots Greys, now part of the Royal Armoured Corps; one regiment of Foot Guards, the Scots Guards; and ten regiments of Infantry of the Line each consisting, at present, of one regular battalion and attached Territorial Army battalions. The Yeomanry and Scout regiments form part of the Territorial Army and have all been mechanised and converted, like the Scots Greys, into units of the Royal Armoured Corps. Each regiment, however, still retains its separate identity and wears its own cap badge. The Lovat Scouts have been amalgamated with the Scottish Horse but have similarily kept their identity. To the purely Scottish regiments, there must be added as part of Scotland's contribution to national defence the many Scottish artillery, anti-aircraft, parachute, engineer, medical and other units.

As a tribute to our kinsmen overseas I have included a section dealing with Scottish units whose members so worthily uphold the military honour of Scotland in different parts of the Commonwealth.

It is not possible in these pages to give more than a brief out-line of the history of each Scottish regiment. The reader who desires to study the history of any corps more fully is advised to read some of the admirable books which have been written around the individual regiments. Most of those books, unfortunately, are now out of print but many of them can be consulted at public libraries.

The story of the sinking of the *Birkenhead* in which members of three famous Scottish regiments were among those involved, has been included as a stirring example of discipline, comradeship and heroism and as typifying the chivalry of the soldier in conditions far removed from those of the battlefield.

The names of the officers and men of Scottish regiments who were awarded the Victoria Cross during the wars of 1914–18 and 1939–45 together with the dates of notification of the awards and the places of the acts of bravery, are shown under the respective regiments.

THE WRECK OF THE " BIRKENHEAD "

On 7th January, 1852, the troopship *Birkenhead* sailed from Cove for the Cape of Good Hope with detachments from the depôts of 10 regiments all under the command of Lieut.-Colonel Seton of the 74th Highlanders.   In all, there were on board 631 persons including the crew and the wives and families of soldiers.   On 26th February when off the Cape and about three miles from land the ship struck a reef of submerged rocks.   The water rushed into the fore part of the ship and many of the soldiers sleeping on the lower deck were drowned.   The remaining soldiers formed up on the quarter deck as on parade.

The Master of the ship, Captain Salmond, in an attempt to get it safely afloat again ordered the engines to be reversed. The result of this, unfortunately, was to hasten the destruction of the ship as it again bumped upon the rocks and a large hole was torn in the bottom.   The situation was now very critical but the soldiers remained quietly in their ranks while the women and children were passed into the boats.   Ten minutes after the *Birkenhead* first struck the rocks she broke in two at the fore-mast and Captain Salmond, convinced that nothing more could be done, advised all to jump over-board and make for the boats.   Colonel Seton, however, pointed out to the men that if they did so they would endanger the lives of the women and children.   Not a soldier left his place and when the ship again broke in two abaft the main-mast, the men were plunged with the wreck into the sea.   An eye-witness relates that " until the vessel disappeared there was not a cry or murmur from the soldiers or sailors."   Those who could swim struck out for the shore but few ever reached it.   Not a single woman or child was lost.

Included among the soldiers who lost their lives were Colonel Seton and 49 members of the 74th (now the 2nd Battalion The Highland Light Infantry), 56 members of the 73rd (now the 2nd Battalion The Black Watch) and 44 of

13

the 91st (now the 1st Battalion The Argyll and Sutherland Highlanders).

Queen Victoria caused a memorial to be erected in Chelsea Hospital recording "the heroic constancy and unbroken discipline" of the troops and the King of Prussia was so impressed with the chivalry and discipline displayed by them that he ordered an account of the incident to be read to every regiment in his service, on three parades.

CAVALRY, GUARDS AND INFANTRY OF THE LINE

THE ROYAL SCOTS GREYS
[2nd Dragoons]

THE ROYAL SCOTS GREYS

OWING to constant disturbances and the threatening attitude of the Covenanters it was considered advisable, in the early part of 1678, to augment the military establishment and accordingly two troops of Dragoons were then added to the regular army, a third being raised later in the year. This was the beginning of the Royal Scots Greys.

In 1681 King Charles II by Royal Warrant authorised the raising of three more troops and formed the six troops into a regiment which was styled the " Royal Regiment of Scots Dragoons." The regiment wore coats of stone grey cloth.

During 1686-7 the regiment was mainly engaged in hunting down persons who had been concerned in Argyll's rebellion but in 1694 it was sent to Flanders where it remained on active service for some four years until the conclusion of the Peace of Ryswick. In 1702 it was again on the Continent as part of the Allied army under Marlborough. At this time the regiment was generally known as the " Scots Greys " and was mounted on grey horses.

In 1704 the Greys won their first battle honour at Blenheim. At Ramillies in 1706 they defeated and captured many of the French Regiment du Roi, the French Grenadier Guards, and in honour of this were given the distinction of wearing the " Grenadier Cap," a tall mitre-shaped head-dress which was later altered to the bearskin cap. Among the wounded at Ramillies was the famous trooper Mrs. Christian Davies (commonly called " Mother Ross ") who had served for four years in the regiment without her sex being discovered. She was awarded a pension of 1s. a day by Queen Anne and on her death on 7th July, 1739, she was buried with full military honours in the cemetery of Chelsea Hospital.

From 1707, when the Parliaments of Scotland and England were united, the regiment was known as " The Royal Regiment of North British Dragoons " and in 1713 it obtained rank as the 2nd Dragoons.

During the rebellion of 1715 the Greys took part in various engagements and won general admiration for their conduct

19

at the battle of Sheriffmuir. In 1742 they were engaged in the War of the Austrian Succession and played a distinguished part at Dettingen, where they captured a white standard belonging to the French household troops, and at Fontenoy. In 1758 the Greys joined the Duke of Brunswick's army in Germany and were present at the battles of Bergen and Minden (1759) and Warburg (1760).

In 1768 the Greys were ordered to wear black bearskin caps with the Thistle within the circle of St. Andrew and the motto " Nemo me impune lacessit " on the front.

The Greys formed part of Ponsonby's Brigade during the Waterloo campaign. On receiving the order to advance at Waterloo they charged to shouts of " Scotland for ever ! " and many of the Gordon Highlanders grasped the stirrups of the Greys to keep up with them. In the charge 2,000 prisoners were taken and Sergeant Ewart of the Greys captured the " Eagle " of the 45th French Infantry. For their services in this campaign the Greys received Royal permission to bear on their guidon the badge of an Eagle and the word " Waterloo." In the Crimean War they were engaged at Sevastopol and took a prominent part in the charge of the Heavy Brigade in front of Balaclava.

In 1877 the title of the regiment was changed to " The Royal Scots Greys."

The regiment served throughout the South African War, winning special commendation in the dash to the relief of Kimberley and at Paardeberg.

In the war of 1914-18 the Greys took part in all the major battles on the Western Front and marched into Germany with the guidon at their head.

At the outbreak of the 1939-45 war, the regiment was in Palestine. In 1941, when half the regiment fought in the Syrian campaign as lorried infantry, the Greys ceased to be " Cavalry of the Line " and joined the Royal Armoured Corps.

The Greys took a leading part in the fighting at Alamein and throughout the 1,500 miles to Tripoli, which they captured with the New Zealand Division. After serving in the Italian campaign, the regiment took part in severe fighting in Normandy and in the pursuit of the enemy across France and the Low Countries into Germany. On 2nd May, 1945, when the port of Wismar on the Baltic was captured, the Greys were the first British troops to meet the Russians.

Since the end of the war of 1939-45 the Greys have remained in Germany.

BATTLE HONOURS :

Blenheim, Ramillies, Oudenarde, Malplaquet, Dettingen, Warburg, Willems, Waterloo, Balaclava, Sevastopol, Relief of Kimberley, Paardeberg, South Africa, 1899-1902.

Retreat from Mons, Marne 1914, Aisne 1914, Ypres 1914, '15, Arras 1917, Amiens, Somme 1918, Hindenburg Line, Pursuit to Mons, France and Flanders 1914-18.

VICTORIA CROSS :

Awards of the Victoria Cross since 1914.

T./Lt.-Col. G.C.T. Keyes, M.C. 19/6/42, Middle East (attd. Special Service Troops).

REGIMENTAL DRESS :

The Greys have no regimental tartan.

The White Horse of Hanover is worn by other ranks on the back of the bearskin.

The White Vandyck worn round the blue patrol cap dates from the end of the 18th century.

REGIMENTAL MARCHES :

Dismounted	....	....	.... " Highland Laddie."
Mounted—Walk	....	....	.... " Garb of Old Gaul."
Trot		....	.... " Keel Row."
Canter		....	.... " Bonnie Dundee."

REGIMENTAL JOURNAL :

The Scots Grey,
Gale and Polden Ltd.
Aldershot

REGIMENTAL ASSOCIATION :

Hon. Secretary : Earl Haig,
　　　Bemersyde, St. Boswells,
　　　　　Roxburghshire.

Branches at Edinburgh, Glasgow, Dundee, Perth, Aberdeen, London and York.

AFFILIATED REGIMENTS :

Canadian
　　2nd/10th Dragoons.
　　The New Brunswick Dragoons.

Australian
　　12th Light Horse Regiment (New England Light Horse).

New Zealand
　　The North Auckland Mounted Rifles.

SCOTS GUARDS

SCOTS GUARDS

The Scots Guards are the second oldest Scottish corps, having been raised in 1642 when King Charles I commissioned Archibald, Marquis of Argyll, to command and send a regiment to Ireland. From the fact that the regiment was chosen to receive the honour of a Royal Commission it is surmised that the King intended it to be used as a guard for his person. One of the officers who sailed with the regiment to Ireland was Major afterwards Sir James Turner, a professional soldier and the original of Sir Walter Scott's Dugald Dalgetty.

The regiment was engaged in operations in Ireland until 1645 and five years later King Charles II selected it to form the nucleus of his Foot Guards. It was present at the battles of Dunbar and Worcester but practically ceased to exist during the following nine years. The regiment was re-created on the restoration of King Charles II and took part in the battles of Rullion Green in 1666 and Bothwell Brig in 1679.

In the War of the League of Augsburg the regiment lost heavily at the battle of Landen (1693) and was present at the capture of Namur (1695).

In 1712 it became known as the " Third Regiment of Foot Guards." From an order issued in 1720 it is interesting to note that the rate for the sale of commissions in the regiment ranged from £150 for Quartermaster to £2,400 for Captain and £5,000 for Lieutenant-Colonel. The purchase of commissions was abolished in 1871.

The regiment took part in the War of the Austrian Succession from 1742 to 1748 and fought at the battles of Dettingen —the last occasion on which a British monarch was present at the front until the War of 1914-18—and Fontenoy. In 1776 two companies formed part of a composite Guards Battalion which was sent to America to assist in quelling the revolt of the American colonies. For its part in the conquest of Egypt in 1801 the regiment, in common with other regiments engaged, was awarded the Sphinx superscribed " Egypt," the first general battle honour to be given in the British Army.

The 2nd Battalion played a distinguished part in the historic defence of the Château of Hougomont at the Battle of Waterloo. It was a party of the Coldstream and 3rd Guards who succeeded in closing the main gate and barring it.

The regiment, then known as the Scots Fusilier Guards, formed part of the Guards Brigade in the Crimean War. The gallantry of the regiment in this campaign is evidenced by the award of five Victoria Crosses.

From about 1785 to the middle of the 19th century the regimental band included three negroes, called time beaters, two of whom carried tambourines and the third Turkish bells. They were dressed in gorgeous Eastern uniforms, heavily braided, and turbans with a plume.

In 1877 Queen Victoria restored to the regiment its old title of Scots Guards.

The regiment further enhanced its reputation in the field during the South African War. It took part in many engagements, including Modder River, Magersfontein and Paardeberg, and displayed tireless endurance in many forced marches during the campaign.

In the war of 1914-18 both battalions saw much hard fighting on the Western Front.

In the 1939-45 war the regiment served in Norway, the Western Desert, North Africa, Italy and North-West Europe.

BATTLE HONOURS :

Namur 1695, Dettingen, Lincelles, Talavera, Barrosa, Fuentes d'Onor, Nive, Peninsula, Waterloo, Alma, Inkerman, Sevastopol, Tel-el-Kebir, Egypt 1882, Suakin 1885, Modder River, South Africa 1899-1902.

Retreat from Mons, Marne 1914, Aisne 1914, Ypres 1914, '17, Festubert 1915, Loos, Somme 1916, '18, Cambrai 1917, '18, Hindenburg Line, France and Flanders, 1914-18.

VICTORIA CROSSES :

Awards of the Victoria Cross since 1914.

Pte. J. Mackenzie, 18/2/15, Rouges Bancs, France.
Sgt. J. McAulay, D.C.M., 11/1/18, Fontaine Notre Dame, France.

L./Sgt. F. McNess, 26/10/16, Nr. Ginchy, France.
2nd/Lt. G. A. B. Rochfort, 1/9/15, Cambrin and La Bassee,
France.
L./Sgt. H. B. Wood, M.M., 14/12/18, St. Python, France.
Capt. The Lord Lyell, 12/8/43, North Africa.

REGIMENTAL TARTAN :

Royal Stewart. The kilt is worn only by the pipers.

REGIMENTAL MARCHES :

Quick March   ....   " Highland Laddie."
Slow March   ....   " Garb of Old Gaul."

REGIMENTAL MAGAZINE :

The Household Brigade Magazine,
Room 80a, Horse Guards,
London, S.W.1.

REGIMENTAL ASSOCIATION :

Scots Guards Association,
Central Office, Birdcage Walk,
London, S.W.1.

Branches in London, Leeds, Merseyside, Preston, Aberdeen,
Ayr, Dundee, Edinburgh, Galloway and Glasgow.

AFFILIATED REGIMENT :

Canadian
The Winnipeg Grenadiers.

THE ROYAL SCOTS
(THE ROYAL REGIMENT)
[1st]

THE ROYAL SCOTS

THE Royal Scots have the distinction of being not only the oldest of the Scottish regiments but the oldest regiment in the British Army.

In 1633 Sir John Hepburn offered to raise a regiment for service with the French in the Thirty Years' War against Austria and Spain. He absorbed what remained of some Scottish companies which had been in the French service since 1590 and some officers and men from other French-Scottish units such as the Scottish Guard and the Scottish Men-at-Arms. In March, 1633, King Charles I granted a warrant authorising men to be raised for the regiment in Scotland and that date is generally taken as the beginning of the regiment as a British regiment. Hepburn's claim of precedence for the regiment over all others in the French service caused some bad feeling and as a hit at mercenaries, one of the senior French regiments nicknamed it " Pontius Pilate's Bodyguard." Sir John Hepburn was only 38 when he was killed at the siege of Saverne in 1636.

In 1684 the title of " The Royal Regiment of Foot " was conferred on it.

The regiment gained its first battle honour in 1680 at Tangier and later was heavily engaged at the battles of Steenkirk and Landen and the siege of Namur, during King William's War of 1689-97. From 1701 to 1713 it took part under Marlborough in the War of the Spanish Succession and in 1745 it was in the first line of attack on the bloody field of Fontenoy. In 1757 the 2nd Battalion sailed for America where, during the Seven Years' War, it gained the battle honours of Louisburg and Havannah.

In the campaign in Holland of 1799 the 2nd Battalion formed part of Sir John Moore's brigade and fought at Egmont-op-Zee, and two years later it participated in Sir Ralph Abercromby's expedition to Egypt.

The regiment was engaged in the Peninsular Wars and rendered gallant service at the battles of Corunna, Busaco, Salamanca, Vittoria, San Sebastian and the Nive. The 3rd Battalion won fresh laurels in the Waterloo campaign and earned high praise for its stout defence at Quatre Bras, where it successfully withstood repeated charges of French cavalry. In the War with the Mahratta princes in 1817 the regiment was the only European unit present at the siege of Nagpore and the battle honour awarded for that event is therefore unique among British regiments. On 4th November, 1843, the transport *Premier*, with the H.Q. and right wing of the 2nd Battalion, was wrecked in a snowstorm in the St. Lawrence estuary, but owing to the fine discipline of the detachment every man, woman and child was safely landed. In the Crimean War, though the regiment enjoyed less opportunities than other regiments of distinguishing itself in action, it gained three more honours, Alma, Inkerman and Sevastopol and Private Prosser won the first Victoria Cross for the regiment.

In 1871 the title was changed to the 1st or " The Royal Scots " Regiment and in 1882 to The Royal Scots (Lothian Regiment).

On the outbreak of the South African War the 1st Battalion had the distinction of being the only battalion in the Army which accounted for every reservist on mobilisation. The regiment fully sustained its reputation in this campaign but owing to the mobility of the enemy it actually lost more men from the hard marches and from enteric fever than from battle casualties.

The regiment expanded during the war of 1914-18 to 35 battalions. It fought on the Western Front, in Gallipoli, Macedonia, Egypt and Palestine and at Archangel and suffered over 11,000 casualties.

In 1920 the old title was restored in reverse when it became The Royal Scots, The Royal Regiment.

In the 1939-45 war the regiment served in France and Belgium till Dunkirk and thereafter in Burma, Italy and North-West Europe.

BATTLE HONOURS :

Tangier 1680, Namur 1695, Blenheim, Ramillies, Oudenarde, Malplaquet, Louisburg, Havannah, Egmont-op-Zee, St. Lucia 1803, Corunna, Busaco, Salamanca, Vittoria, San Sebastian, Nive, Peninsula, Niagara, Waterloo, Nagpore, Maheidpoor, Ava, Alma, Inkerman, Sevastopol, Taku Forts, Pekin 1860, South Africa 1899-1902.

Le Cateau, Marne 1914, '18, Ypres 1915, '17, '18, Loos, Somme 1916, '18, Arras 1917, '18, Lys, Struma, Gallipoli 1915-16, Palestine 1917-18.

Victoria Crosses :

Awards of the Victoria Cross since 1914.

Pte. R. Dunsire, 18/11/15, Hill 70, France.
L./Cpl. R. E. Elcock, M.M., 26/12/18, St. Catherine, France.
Lt. D. S. McGregor, 14/12/18, Hoogmolen, Belgium.
Pte. H. McIver, M.M., 15/11/18, Courcelles-le-Comte, France.
Pte. H. H. Robson, 18/2/15, Nr. Kemmel, France.
T./Capt. H. Reynolds, M.C., 8/11/17, nr. Frezenburg, Belgium.

Regimental Tartan :

Hunting Stewart. The 7/9th (T.A.) Battalion only is kilted.
The pipers wear the Royal Stewart tartan, having had that honour conferred on them by King George V on the occasion of the Tercentenary Parade in 1933.

Regimental Marches :

" Dumbarton's Drums."
Slow March—" The Garb of Old Gaul."

" Blue Bonnets " is played by the pipers when marching into barracks, etc.
The regiment march past to " The Daughter of the Regiment " when Royalty are on parade. This commemorates the fact that Queen Victoria was born in the regiment, her father, the Duke of Kent, having been Colonel of the regiment at the time of her birth.

Regimental Journal :

The Thistle,
   Glencorse Barracks, Milton Bridge, Midlothian.

C

REGIMENTAL ASSOCIATIONS :

> (a) The Royal Scots Association,
>> c/o The Royal Scots Club,
>>> 30 Abercromby Place, Edinburgh, 3.

> Branches at Edinburgh, Glasgow, London and Manchester.

> (b) The Royal Scots Benevolent Fund,
>> c/o The Royal Scots Club,
>>> 30 Abercromby Place, Edinburgh, 3.

AFFILIATED REGIMENT :

> The Canadian Scottish Regiment (Highlanders) (Princess Mary's).

THE ROYAL SCOTS FUSILIERS
[21st]

THE ROYAL SCOTS FUSILIERS

THE regiment was raised in 1678 when a commission was issued to Charles Erskine, fifth Earl of Mar, as Colonel of a new foot regiment which soon became popularly known as the " Earl of Mar's Greybreeks." It was not until 1685 that it became in the full sense Fusilier. Some nine years later it was ranked the 21st Regiment of Foot.

The regiment's first foreign campaign was from 1689 to 1697 in Flanders, where it distinguished itself at Steenkirk and Landen. It suffered heavily in the great battles of Marlborough during the War of the Spanish Succession, more especially at Blenheim, and was one of the regiments granted the right to wear the White Horse of Hanover. The White Horse is still worn by the Drum Major on his belt. About 1713 the regiment became a royal regiment, being known as the Royal North British Fusiliers.

The Fusiliers were again in action at the battle of Dettingen in 1743 under the command of Sir Andrew Agnew of Lochnaw, probably the most memorable and best loved figure in the regiment's history. It was he who at Dettingen bade his men " Dinna fire till ye see the whites o' their een."

The regiment went to America during the American Revolution and Burgoyne's surrender at Saratoga in 1777 saw the virtual end of the 21st. By 1782 it was reconstituted and formed part of the expedition to the West Indies in 1793.

A 2nd battalion was raised in 1804. It took the field for the first and only time at Bergen-op-Zoom in Holland in 1814 and was disbanded in 1816.

In 1854 the 21st embarked for the Crimea where it won much renown for its stubborn defence at the battle of Inkerman.

In 1877 the regiment was given royal authority to assume the name of the 21st Royal Scots Fusiliers, and in 1881 became the 1st and 2nd Battalions Royal Scots Fusiliers. At the same time the uniform was altered from the ordinary line tunic to the doublet with tartan trews.

The present 2nd Battalion, which was raised in 1858, had its baptism of fire in the Zululand and Transvaal campaigns of 1879-1881. The battalion played a distinguished part in some of the hardest fighting of the 1899-1902 campaign in South Africa where the first Victoria Cross in the history of the regiment was won by Private Ravenhill.

In 1902 permission was finally granted to the regiment to wear again a white plume on the right side of their Fusilier caps. The plume had been abolished about 1860.

In the war of 1914-18 the regiment expanded to 18 battalions and was represented in every main action on the Western Front. They were also at Gallipoli, in the Palestine campaign till Jerusalem fell and at Salonika. The Right Hon. Winston Churchill was Colonel of the 6th Battalion from December, 1915, to May, 1916.

The campaigns in which battalions of the Fusiliers took part during the 1939-45 war included France and Belgium 1940, Madagascar 1942, Italy 1943, Burma 1944 and North-West Europe 1944.

The regiment was presented with the Freedom of the Royal Burgh of Ayr in June 1945, and has the right to march through the town with drums beating, bayonets fixed and Colours flying.

BATTLE HONOURS:

Blenheim, Ramillies, Oudenarde, Malplaquet, Dettingen, Martinique 1794, Bladensburg, Alma, Inkerman, Sevastopol, South Africa 1879, Burma 1885-87, Tirah, Relief of Ladysmith, South Africa 1899-1902.

Mons, Marne 1914, Ypres 1914, '17, '18, Somme 1916, '18, Arras 1917, '18, Lys, Hindenburg Line, Doiran 1917, '18, Gallipoli 1915-16, Palestine 1917-18.

VICTORIA CROSSES:

Awards of the Victoria Cross since 1914.

2nd/Lt. S. H. P. Boughey, 13/2/18, El Burf, Palestine.
Sgt. T. Caldwell, 6/1/19, Oudenarde, Belgium.
2nd/Lt. J. M. Craig, 2/8/17, Egypt.
Pte. D. R. Lauder, 13/1/17, Cape Helles, Gallipoli.
Fus. D. Donnini, 20/3/45, North-West Europe.

REGIMENTAL TARTAN :

The 42nd tartan was worn until 1948, when H.M. The King gave his approval to the wearing of the Hunting Erskine, the family tartan of the Earls of Mar.

The pipers wear the ceremonial Erskine tartan. Permission to wear this tartan was granted by King George V in 1928 to commemorate the 250th anniversary of the raising of the regiment by the 5th Earl of Mar.

REGIMENTAL MARCHES :

Band   ....   " The British Grenadiers."
Pipes   ....   " Highland Laddie."

REGIMENTAL JOURNAL :

The Journal of The Royal Scots Fusiliers,
    The Barracks,
        Ayr.

REGIMENTAL ASSOCIATION :

The Royal Scots Fusiliers Association,
    Gordon Chambers,
        90 Mitchell Street,
            Glasgow, C.1.

Branches at Edinburgh, Dundee, Kilmarnock, Ayr and Greenock.

AFFILIATED REGIMENTS :

Canadian
    The Scots Fusiliers of Canada.

Australian
    23rd/21st Battalion. (The City of Geelong Regiment and The Victorian Rangers.)

South African
    Prince Alfred's Guard.

THE KING'S OWN
SCOTTISH BORDERERS
[25th]

THE KING'S OWN SCOTTISH BORDERERS

THE regiment was raised in Edinburgh in 1689 by the Earl of Leven under a commission given by a Committee of the Convention of Estates. It was originally named " Leven's " or The Edinburgh Regiment and about 1744 was numbered the 25th Foot.

The regiment fought its first battle in 1689 at the Pass of Killiecrankie where it was one of the only two regiments that did not run away before the charge of the Highlanders. It was next in action in the campaign in Ireland of 1691 and was present at the sieges of Athlone, Galway and Limerick. During the war of the League of Augsburg from 1692-97 the regiment was in Flanders and won its first battle honour at Namur in 1695. It was at Namur that the discovery was made that the French could fire from their rifles with bayonets fixed. Up to that time when bayonets had been fixed firing was impossible.

In the war of the Austrian Succession the 25th fought at Fontenoy and Ath in 1745 and surrendered with honours of war at the latter place. After being recalled to Scotland for Culloden, the regiment returned to Flanders and was present at the battle of Bergen-op-Zoom. It was again on the Continent during the Seven Years' War of 1756-63 and took part in many engagements, including Minden and Warburg.

In 1782 the title was changed to the " Sussex Regiment," due it is believed to the fact that the commanding officer was a brother of the Duke of Richmond whose chief seat was in Sussex.

During the war of the French Revolution it supplied detachments for service as marines, some being present at the victory over the main French fleet off Brest in 1794. After service in the West Indies the regiment was engaged in 1799 in Holland and formed the advance guard in the action of Egmont-op-Zee. In 1801 it took part in the expedition to Egypt and for its share in this campaign bears on its colours the Sphinx superscribed " Egypt."

In 1805 the regiment became "The King's Own Borderers" and as a royal regiment its facings were changed from yellow to blue.

It was again on service in the West Indies from 1807 to 1817 and during that period it was at the capture of Martinique and Guadaloupe. The 1st Battalion was engaged in the Second Afghan War of 1878-80 and the 2nd Battalion, which had been raised in 1859, was in action in Egypt in 1888 and played a leading part in the relief of Chitral in 1895. The 1st Battalion served in the South African campaign of 1900-02.

On the army reorganisation in 1881 it was proposed that the regiment should be called "The York Regiment King's Own Borderers," but after strong protests the proposal was dropped. In 1887 the regiment was officially designated "The King's Own Scottish Borderers."

In the war of 1914-18 it was in action on the Western Front, Gallipoli and Palestine. All the battalions of the regiment serving on the Western Front were engaged in the battle of the Somme of 1916 and the battle of Arras of April 1917.

In the 1939-45 war the 1st Battalion served in France and Flanders till Dunkirk and, after the invasion of Normandy, in North-West Europe; the 2nd Battalion in Burma; and the 4th, 5th and 6th Battalions in the North-West Europe campaign. The 7th Battalion was airborne and fought at Arnhem.

The regiment has the privilege of beating up for recruits in Edinburgh without first obtaining the permission of the Lord Provost, and the right to march through the city with bayonets fixed and colours flying.

BATTLE HONOURS :

Namur 1695, Minden, Egmont-op-Zee, Martinique 1809, Afghanistan 1878-80, Chitral, Tirah, Paardeberg, South Africa 1900-02.

Mons, Aisne 1914, Ypres 1914, '15, '17, '18, Loos, Somme 1916, '18, Arras 1917, '18, Soissonnais-Ourcq, Hindenburg Line, Gallipoli 1915-16, Gaza.

VICTORIA CROSSES :

Awards of the Victoria Cross since 1914.

A/C.Q.M.S. W. H. Grimbaldeston, 14/9/17, Wijdendrift, Belgium.

Piper D. Laidlaw, 18/11/15, Nr. Loos and Hill 70, France.

A/Sgt. L. McGuffie, 14/12/18, Wytschaete, Belgium.

A/C.S.M. J. Skinner, 14/9/17, Wijdendrift, Belgium.

REGIMENTAL TARTAN :

Leslie Tartan.

The pipers of all battalions, except the 4th, wear the Royal Stewart tartan. The 4th Battalion pipers wear the " Shepherd's Plaid."

REGIMENTAL MARCH :

" Blue Bonnets."

REGIMENTAL JOURNAL :

The Borderers Chronicle,
  The Barracks,
    Berwick-on-Tweed.

REGIMENTAL ASSOCIATION :

K.O.S.B. Association,
  The Barracks,
    Berwick-on-Tweed.

Branches at Edinburgh, Glasgow, Galashiels, Hawick, Kirkconnel, Berwick-on-Tweed, Dumfries, Wigtown, Sanquhar, London, Selkirk, Jedburgh, Newcastleton, Leeds, and Ontario, Canada.

AFFILIATED REGIMENTS :

Canadian
  The St. John Fusiliers (M.G.).

Australian
  25th Battalion (The Darling Downs Regiment).

THE CAMERONIANS (SCOTTISH RIFLES)
[26th-90th]

THE CAMERONIANS (SCOTTISH RIFLES)

THE 1st Battalion was formerly the 26th Cameronians and the 2nd Battalion the 90th Perthshire Light Infantry.

The " Cameronians " honour in their title the memory of Richard Cameron, one of the most notable of the Covenanters. It was originally intended that the regiment should be organised in some degree on the model of a Presbyterian congregation, that each company should provide an elder and that each man should carry a Bible.

The 26th Cameronians were raised in 1689 under the leadership of the Earl of Angus and soon showed their mettle against the followers of the Stuarts in the heroic defence of Dunkeld where, 1,200 strong, they repulsed with great loss four times their number. They took part in the capture of Namur in 1695 and some years later under the famous Duke of Marlborough they rendered gallant service in Flanders and won special renown at Blenheim. In 1809 the Cameronians were with Sir John Moore at the battle of Corunna, a victory which crowned a masterly retreat in the depth of winter. They further distinguished themselves in China in 1840, particularly at the capture of Amoy, where they were the first to mount the walls.

In 1794 the 90th Perthshire Light Infantry (nicknamed " The Perthshire Greybreeks ") was formed by Mr. Thomas Graham, afterwards General Lord Lynedoch. The 90th won its first distinction in Sir Ralph Abercromby's expedition to Egypt in 1801. The battle honour of " Mandora " gained in that campaign is borne by only one other regiment of the British Army, the 92nd (now the 2nd Battalion The Gordon Highlanders), although upwards of 20 infantry regiments, besides several of cavalry, took part in the action. Some years later the 90th was engaged in the capture of Martinique and Guadaloupe, two valuable West Indian islands. At Guadaloupe the regiment captured the Eagle of the 80th French Regiment, one of the first Eagles to be taken by a British regiment. After serving with distinction in the Crimea, the 90th added to its reputation in the Indian Mutiny by the many acts of individual bravery performed by officers and men. No fewer than six Victoria Crosses were won by members of the regiment.

In 1881 the 26th and 90th were amalgamated under the title of " The Cameronians (Scottish Rifles)." On becoming a rifle corps the regiment ceased to carry colours, and all battle honours are now borne on the appointments only.

It saw much service in the Boer War and formed part of the force which, after much hardship, brought relief to their besieged comrades at Ladysmith.

In the war of 1914-18 the regiment consisted of 27 battalions and, as its battle honours attest, added new lustre to its name on the Western Front, and in Macedonia, Gallipoli and Palestine.

In the 1939-45 war the 1st Battalion took part in the Burma campaign of 1942, returning there in 1944 with Wingate's Chindits, the 2nd Battalion was at Dunkirk 1940, Madagascar 1942, the Sicily landing and later in France, while other battalions participated, after D-day, in the North-West Europe campaign.

The regiment holds the unique honour of having given to its country two Commanders-in-Chief, Lord Hill and Viscount Wolseley, and two Field Marshals, Viscount Wolseley and Sir Evelyn Wood, V.C. In the 1939-45 war it could boast of having produced seven General Officers, including General Sir Thomas Riddell - Webster and General Sir Richard O'Connor.

BATTLE HONOURS :

> Blenheim, Ramillies, Oudenarde, Malplaquet, Mandora, Corunna, Martinique 1809, Guadaloupe 1810, South Africa 1846-7, Sevastopol, Lucknow, Abyssinia, South Africa 1877-8-9, Relief of Ladysmith, South Africa 1899-1902.

> Mons, Marne 1914, '18, Neuve Chapelle, Loos, Somme 1916, '18, Ypres 1917, '18, Hindenburg Line, Macedonia 1915-18, Gallipoli 1915-16, Palestine 1917-18.

VICTORIA CROSSES :

> Awards of the Victoria Cross since 1914.

> A/Sgt. J. Erskine, 5/8/16, Givenchy, France.

Pte. H. May, 19/4/15, La Boutillerie, France.
Pte. J. Towers, 6/1/19, Mericourt, France.

REGIMENTAL TARTAN, ETC. :

Douglas tartan. It is worn by all ranks, including the band.

The pipers of the 1st Battalion wear a distinctive badge of the Mullet or Star with a scroll below bearing the name " The Cameronians."

The sporrans and dirks of the pipers of the 2nd Battalion carry a reproduction of the coat of arms of the City of Perth.

When swords were worn before the 1939-45 war, the officers did not carry a basket-hilted broadsword as in other Lowland regiments but wore a rifle sword.

REGIMENTAL MARCHES :

Band	....	....	....	" Within a mile of Edinburgh toun."
Pipers—1st Battalion		....		" Kenmuir's on and awa'."
2nd Battalion		....		" The Athol Highlanders."

REGIMENTAL JOURNAL :

The Covenanter,
    Winston Barracks,
        Lanark.

REGIMENTAL ASSOCIATION :

The Barracks,
    Hamilton,
Branch in London.

REGIMENTAL CLUBS :

4 Lynedoch Place, Glasgow, C.3.
5 St. Vincent Street, Edinburgh, 3.

AFFILIATED REGIMENTS :

Canadian

The Perth Regiment (M.G.).

Australian

26th Battalion (The Logan and Albert Regiment).

New Zealand

The Otago Regiment.

South African.

Witwatersrand Rifles.

THE BLACK WATCH
(ROYAL HIGHLAND REGIMENT)
[42nd-73rd]

THE BLACK WATCH

ABOUT 1725 certain Highland chieftains were commissioned to raise bodies of their clansmen, known as Independent Companies, to keep order in their different localities. It was formerly believed that the men of those companies wore the tartans of their company commanders and that the name " Black " was derived from the dark colours of the tartans but more recent researches have indicated that the companies did not wear the tartan of their commanders and that the " Black " referred to their duty of suppressing "black-mail." In 1739 the companies were formed into the 43rd Regiment. In 1749 the number was changed, the regiment becoming known as the 42nd or Highland Regiment, and nine years later the title of " Royal " was conferred.

The regiment went into action for the first time in 1745 at the battle of Fontenoy, and from 1758 to 1767 was engaged in operations in America. It returned to America during the American War of Independence (1776-83) and it is interesting to note that the 42nd is the only existing Highland regiment which served in this and the other campaigns mentioned.

In 1795 the 42nd adopted the Red Hackle, which is still worn in the balmoral bonnet in place of a badge.

It was in action in 1801 in Egypt and participated in the battle of Alexandria, one of the hardest battles in which the regiment has ever taken part. One of the highlights of the battle was the capture of the standard of Napoleon's " Invincible Legion " by Major Stirling of the 42nd. The 42nd held the post of honour as rearguard in the retreat to Corunna in 1809 and gained in all nine battle honours for its part in the Peninsular War. For its services at Quatre Bras and Waterloo it received special mention in the Duke of Wellington's dispatch on these battles. The 42nd, with the 79th and 93rd Highlanders, formed the famous Highland Brigade in the Crimean War. During its service in the Indian Mutiny the regiment captured its well-known gong, which ever since has tolled the hours in every station and country where the Black Watch has been quartered.

In 1861 Queen Victoria conferred on the regiment the

name " The Black Watch " in addition to its title of Royal Highland Regiment.

The present 2nd Battalion, which was embodied at Perth in 1781, was formed into a separate regiment in 1786 and numbered the 73rd. It took part in the capture and subsequent siege of Mangalore in 1783 and in the Mysore campaign of 1791-92. In 1809 the 73rd, together with several other Highland regiments, were ordered to discontinue the Highland dress which was considered a detriment to recruiting. It was engaged at Quatre Bras and two days later at Waterloo, where its losses in killed and wounded amounted to 289. In 1852, during the second Kaffir War, 56 members of the 73rd were drowned in the tragic wreck of the *Birkenhead*. In 1881 the 73rd returned to its parent regiment, the 42nd once more as its 2nd Battalion.

The regiment took part in the Egyptian campaign of 1882 and distinguished itself as part of the Highland Brigade at Tel-el-Kebir. It also saw much hard fighting in the South African War, especially at Magersfontein, where the 2nd Battalion suffered severely, and at Paardeberg.

During the war of 1914-18 the regiment consisted of 27 battalions and fought in France and Flanders, Macedonia, Egypt, Mesopotamia and Palestine. Sixty-eight battle honours were awarded to the regiment for the 1914-18 war, and of these, ten were selected for emblazoning on the Colour.

In the 1939-45 war it served in almost all theatres of war, including the Middle East, North Africa, Italy, Burma and North-West Europe. Three battalions served with the 51st Highland Division.

BATTLE HONOURS :

Guadeloupe 1759, Martinique 1762, Havannah, North America 1763-64, Mangalore, Mysore, Seringapatam, Corunna, Busaco, Fuentes d'Onor, Pyrenees, Nivelle, Nive, Orthes, Toulouse, Peninsula, Waterloo, South Africa 1846-47, 1851-2-3, Alma, Sevastopol, Lucknow, Ashantee, 1873-4, Tel-el-Kebir, Egypt 1882, 1884, Kirbekan, Nile 1884-5, Paardeberg, South Africa 1899-1902.

Marne 1914, '18, Ypres 1914, '17, '18, Loos, Somme 1916,' 18, Arras 1917, '18, Lys, Hindenburg Line, Doiran 1917, Megiddo, Kut al Amara 1917.

Victoria Crosses :

Awards of the Victoria Cross since 1914.

A/Lt.-Col. L. P. Evans, D.S.O., 26/11/17, Zonnebeke, Belgium.

L./Cpl. D. Findlay, 29/6/15, Rue du Bois, France.

Pte. C. Melvin, 26/11/17, Mesopotamia.

Cpl. J. Ripley, 29/6/15, Rue du Bois, France.

Regimental Tartan :

The 42nd (Black Watch) tartan. It is worn by all battalions and by the band except the pipers. The pipers wear the Royal Stewart tartan.

The pleats of the kilt worn by The Black Watch are rounded, whereas the kilts of other Highland regiments have flat pleats.

Regimental March :

" Highland Laddie."

Regimental Journal :

The Red Hackle,
Queen's Barracks,
Perth.

Regimental Association :

The Black Watch Association,
Queen's Barracks,
Perth.

Branches at Aberdeen, Arbroath, Blairgowrie, Cowdenbeath, Crieff, Dunblane, Dundee, Dunfermline, Edinburgh, Glasgow, Kirkcaldy, London, Montrose, Newcastle, Perth and St. Andrews.

There are also branches at Toronto, Brantford and Montreal, Canada ; Sydney, Australia ; and Bulawayo, Southern Rhodesia.

AFFILIATED REGIMENTS :
>The Tyneside Scottish.

Canadian
>The Black Watch (Royal Highland Regiment) of Canada.
>The Lanark and Renfrew Scottish Regiment (Highlanders).
>The Prince Edward Island Highlanders.

Australian
>30th Battalion (The New South Wales Scottish Regiment).
>42nd Battalion (The Capricornia Regiment).

New Zealand
>The New Zealand Scottish Regiment.

South African
>Transvaal Scottish.

THE HIGHLAND LIGHT INFANTRY
(CITY OF GLASGOW REGIMENT)
[71st-74th]

THE HIGHLAND LIGHT INFANTRY

THE 71st was originally raised in 1777 as the 73rd Highland Regiment (Macleod's Highlanders) by John Mackenzie, commonly called John, Lord Macleod. He was imprisoned in the Tower of London for taking part in the Jacobite Rising of 1745, but was released on account of his youth and went to Sweden where he rose to the rank of General in the Swedish Army. On the outbreak of the American War of Independence he returned home and was granted permission by King George III to raise a regiment. The regiment wore a kilt of the military or 42nd pattern with buff and white lines and feathered bonnet with red and white hackle. In 1786 the title was changed to the 71st, in 1809 to the 71st Highland Light Infantry and in 1881 to the 1st Battalion Highland Light Infantry.

The 74th was raised in 1787 and styled " The 74th Highland Regiment of Foot." The uniform was the full Highland dress, the tartan being similar to that of the 42nd Highlanders (now The Black Watch). In 1881 the 74th became the 2nd Battalion Highland Light Infantry.

The 71st in 1834 adopted tartan trews in place of the kilt which was unsuitable for Light Infantry. The 74th discontinued the wearing of the kilt whilst on service in India soon after its formation and subsequently practically lost its identity as a Highland regiment. In 1845 it again became a Highland corps wearing tartan trews and diced shako. The tartan was that of the military or 42nd pattern with a white stripe, which tartan it wore until the " linking " in 1881 with the 71st.

In 1947 approval was given to the regiment once more adopting the dress of a kilted regiment. The tartan is the military or 42nd with red and white line, now known as Mackenzie.

The 71st served with distinction throughout the arduous campaign in the Carnatic against Hyder Ali until the conclusion of peace in 1784. Eight years later the 71st and 74th were both in action in India and at the assault upon Seringapatam in 1792 they fought together for the first time. In

1803 the 74th was presented with special honorary colours to commemorate its most distinguished part in the great battle of Assaye, one of the most decisive in Indian history. In this action every officer present with the regiment, except Quartermaster James Grant, and 384 of the 500 men who formed for battle, were either killed or wounded.

The 71st was specially selected by King George III in 1809 to be added to the chosen band of Light Infantry regiments which then formed a *corps d'élite* of the Army in the First Peninsular War. Both the 71st and 74th took a prominent part in the battles of the second campaign in the Peninsula from 1810 to 1814. Piper McLaughlin, one of the regimental pipers of the 74th, played his pipes at the head of the advance at the storming of Badajos until the music was stopped by a shot through the bag, and the next year, at the battle of Vittoria, he had both legs shot off whilst playing behind the Colours but continued playing until he died.

The 71st formed part of the famous Light Brigade at the battle of Waterloo and at one period of the battle the Duke of Wellington himself took refuge in a square of the 71st during a French charge. The 71st also participated in many engagements during the Indian Mutiny.

The 71st and 74th were amalgamated in 1881 into one regiment and in the following year the 2nd Battalion took a leading part in the decisive battle of Tel-el-Kebir. The 1st Battalion served in South Africa throughout the campaign of 1899-1902 and as part of the Highland Brigade suffered severe losses at Magersfontein.

During the war of 1914-18, when 26 battalions were raised, the regiment saw much service on the Western Front, and in Gallipoli, Egypt, Palestine, Mesopotamia and North Russia.

In the 1939-45 war it was in action in France and Belgium (1940), Eritrea, Western Desert, Sicily, Italy, Adriatic and North-West Europe.

The regiment received the Freedom of the City of Glasgow on 16th March, 1948.

BATTLE HONOURS :

Carnatic, Hindoostan, Sholinghur, Mysore, Seringapatam, Cape of Good Hope 1806, Roleia, Vimiera, Corunna,

Busaco, Fuentes d'Onor, Ciudad Rodrigo, Badajoz, Almaraz, Salamanca, Vittoria, Pyrenees, Nivelle, Nive, Orthes, Toulouse, Peninsula, Waterloo, South Africa 1851-2-3, Sevastopol, Central India, Tel-el-Kebir, Egypt 1882, Modder River, South Africa 1899-1902.

Mons, Ypres 1914, '15, '17, '18, Loos, Somme 1916, '18, Arras 1917, '18, Hindenburg Line, Gallipoli 1915-16, Palestine 1917-18, Mesopotamia 1916-18, Archangel 1919.

Victoria Crosses :

Awards of the Victoria Cross since 1914.
A/Lt.-Col. W. H. Anderson, 3/5/18, Bois Favieres, France.
L./Cpl. W. Angus, 29/6/15, Givenchy, France.
Lt. W. L. Brodie, 12/12/14, Becelaere, Belgium.
L./Cpl. J. B. Hamilton, 26/11/17, Ypres/Menin Rd., France.
Cpl. D. F. Hunter, 23/10/18, Moeuvres, France.
Sgt. J. T. Turnbull, 25/11/16, Authville, France.
Pte. G. Wilson, 5/12/14, Nr. Verneuil, France.
T/Major F. G. Blaker, M.C., 26/9/44, Burma.

Regimental Tartan :

Mackenzie tartan. In 1947 approval was given for the regiment to adopt the dress of a kilted regiment and in January 1948, new patterns of dress were authorised, including a kilt of the Mackenzie tartan. The new patterns will apply to all battalions, including the 1st Battalion The Glasgow Highlanders, H.L.I. (formerly 9th H.L.I.), who at present wear the Black Watch tartan and a badge similar in design to the Black Watch badge.

Regimental Marches :

March Past in Column	....	....	" Blue Bonnets."
March Past in Close Column	....	" Highland Laddie."
Marching into Barracks	....	....	" Scotland the Brave."

Regimental Journal :

The H.L.I. Chronicle,
    Maryhill Barracks,
    Glasgow, N.W.

REGIMENTAL ASSOCIATION :
> 113 St. Vincent Street,
>> Glasgow, C.2.
> Branches at Edinburgh and London.

AFFILIATED REGIMENT :
> *Canadian*
>> The Highland Light Infantry of Canada

THE SEAFORTH HIGHLANDERS
(ROSS-SHIRE BUFFS,
THE DUKE OF ALBANY'S)
[72nd-78th]

THE SEAFORTH HIGHLANDERS

THE regiment as at present constituted was formed by the amalgamation in 1881 of the old 78th or Seaforth's Highlanders, later the 72nd Highlanders (Duke of Albany's Own), and the 78th or Ross-shire Buffs. The 72nd became the present 1st Battalion and the 78th the 2nd Battalion.

The old 78th was raised in 1778 by the Earl of Seaforth and was designated " Seaforth's Highlanders " and numbered the 78th Regiment. In 1778 it was sent to the Channel Islands and while there repulsed several French attempts to land on the islands. It was next in action in India in 1783 against the fort of Cuddalore in the Carnatic, where for the following 15 years it served in the campaigns against the Sultan of Mysore.

In 1786 the regiment was renumbered the 72nd, the old number of 78th, curiously enough, being allotted in 1793 to the present 2nd Battalion. In 1806 the 72nd was included in the force which under Sir David Baird seized the Cape of Good Hope and in 1810 it took part in the capture of Mauritius. In 1809 it ceased to be on the Highland establishment and assumed the uniform of the Line, but in 1823 it again became a Highland regiment, this time with trews instead of kilts. In the latter year the title was changed to " The 72nd or the Duke of Albany's Own Highlanders."

The 72nd was with the Highland Brigade, under Sir Colin Campbell, at the siege and capture of Sevastopol in 1855 and two years later it led the assault at the storming of Kotah during the Indian Mutiny. The 72nd took part in the Afghan War of 1878 and was congratulated on its gallantry at the assault and capture of Peiwar Kotal. It led the attack at the battle of Charasiah in 1879 and participated in the famous march to Kandahar in the following year.

The 78th was raised in 1793 by Francis Humberstone Mackenzie of Seaforth, afterwards Lord Seaforth, and had its first experience of active service in 1794 in the Netherlands. In the latter year a 2nd battalion of the 78th was raised and granted the title of " The Ross-shire Buffs." This battalion took part in the capture of the Cape of Good Hope in 1795 and shortly afterwards was amalgamated with the first 78th. A 2nd Battalion was again raised in 1804 but after fighting at the battle of Maida (1806) and in Egypt (1807) and Holland (1814), was united with the 1st Battalion in 1816.

The 78th suffered heavily in the battle of Assaye in 1803, and for its services was awarded the honour of the Elephant superscribed " Assaye," and was one of three regiments presented by the East India Company with a third, or honorary colour. In November 1816, the regiment was wrecked on its way to India and was marooned on the lonely island of Preparis for nearly a month. During the Indian Mutiny the 78th was present at the taking of Cawnpore and formed part of the force which relieved Lucknow on 23rd September 1857, remaining at the Residency until it was finally relieved on 17th November. No fewer than eight V.C.s were awarded to members of the 78th for gallantry in the Mutiny campaign.

In 1881 the 72nd and 78th were united as the " Seaforth Highlanders." In 1882 the 1st Battalion again assumed the kilt and from that date the uniforms of the two battalions have been identical.

In 1882 the 1st Battalion assisted in the suppression of the mutiny of the Egyptian Army and took part in the battle of Tel-el-Kebir. It further distinguished itself at Atbara and Omdurman in 1898. During the South African War the 2nd Battalion served throughout the campaign as part of the Highland Brigade.

In the war of 1914-18 the regiment consisted of 19 battalions and saw much hard fighting on the Western Front, Mesopotamia, Macedonia and Palestine.

In the 1939-45 war it served in almost every theatre of war including France and Belgium, Middle East, North Africa, Sicily, Italy, North-West Europe, Java and Malaya.

The Seaforths are the only Highland regiment to have a Gaelic motto " Cuidich'n Righ " (" Help the King ") on its colours and regimental badge.

BATTLE HONOURS :

Carnatic, Hindoostan, Mysore, Cape of Good Hope 1806, Maida, Java, South Africa 1835, Sevastopol, Koosh-ab, Persia, Lucknow, Central India, Peiwar Kotal, Charasiah, Kabul 1879, Kandahar 1880, Afghanistan 1878-80, Tel-el-

Kebir, Egypt 1882, Chitral, Atbara, Khartoum, Paardeberg, South Africa 1899-1902.

Marne 1914, '18, Ypres 1915, '17, '18, Loos, Somme 1916, '18, Arras 1917, '18, Vimy 1917, Cambrai 1917, '18, Valenciennes, Palestine 1918, Baghdad.

Victoria Crosses:

Awards of the Victoria Cross since 1914.
Sgt. A. Edwards, 14/9/17, Ypres, Belgium.
Lt. D. Mackintosh, 8/6/17, Fampoux, France.
L./Cpl. R. McBeath, 11/1/18, Cambrai, France.
Sgt. J. Meikle, M.M., 16/9/18, Nr. Marfaux, France.
Dmr. W. Ritchie, 9/9/16, Beaumont Hamel, France.
L./Sgt. T. Steele, 8/6/17, Sanna-i-Yat, Mesopotamia.
Cpl. S. W. Ware, 26/9/16, Sanna-i-Yat, Mesopotamia.

Regimental Tartan:

MacKenzie tartan. It is worn by all battalions, the 5th Territorial Battalion which formerly wore the Sutherland tartan and badge having been disbanded.
Band, pipers and drums wear the same tartan.

Regimental Marches:

Quarter Column—Band   ....   " Blue Bonnets."
March Past—Pipers   ....   " Pibroch o' Donuil Dhu."

Regimental Journal:

Cabar Feidh,
    Fort George,
        Inverness-shire.

Regimental Association:

Fort George.

Branches at Dingwall, Wick, Nairn, Elgin, Dundee, Edinburgh, Glasgow, Kilmarnock, Derby and London.

Affiliated Regiments:

Canadian

The Seaforth Highlanders of Canada.
The Pictou Highlanders.

THE GORDON HIGHLANDERS
[75th-92nd]

THE GORDON HIGHLANDERS

THE Gordon Highlanders were raised in 1794 by the 4th Duke of Gordon whose wife, the beautiful Duchess Jean, is reputed to have promised a kiss to all recruits who " took the shilling." They were originally numbered the 100th Regiment, but in 1798 became the 92nd, under which number they were known until their amalgamation with the 75th Regiment in 1881. On the amalgamation, the 75th became the 1st Battalion The Gordon Highlanders and the 92nd the 2nd Battalion.

The 92nd's first campaign abroad was against Holland in 1799. At the battle of Egmont-op-Zee General, afterwards Sir John Moore, was carried wounded off the field by two Gordons but a reward of £20 offered by him on his recovery was never claimed. When General Moore was created a Knight of the Bath in 1804 he chose as one of the supporters of his coat-of-arms the figure of a Gordon Highlander.

The regiment next saw service in Egypt, where it distinguished itself at the battle of Mandora in 1801. The Cameronians and Gordons are the only regiments which have this historic name among their honours. The regiment was also awarded eight battle honours for its gallant services in the Peninsular War.

In 1815, at the battle of Waterloo, there took place one of the most glorious incidents in the history of the regiment. Just as the Gordons were about to charge, the Scots Greys came up and with shouts of " Scotland for ever " both regiments charged together. Many of the Highlanders grasped the Greys' legs and stirrup-leathers as they swept forward and in three minutes the French column was completely shattered. In 1872 the regiment adopted the Stag's Head, with the motto " Bydand," as its crest, replacing the Sphinx with the word " Egypt," which had been in use since 1805. The 92nd served throughout the Afghan War of 1878-80 and shared in the hardships of the famous march from Kabul to Kandahar.

The 75th was raised in 1787 and was popularly known as Abercromby's Highlanders. The regiment went into action for the first time in the campaign of 1790 against the Sultan of

Mysore and also took part in the later campaign of 1799. It rendered distinguished service in the Indian Mutiny and formed part of the force which relieved Lucknow.

After the amalgamation of the 75th and 92nd in 1881 the Gordons took part in the Egyptian Wars of 1882-84. Some ten years later they were fighting on the North-West Frontier of India and it was at Dargai in 1897 that Piper Findlater, V.C., though shot through both ankles sat up under a heavy fire and played the regimental march to speed the charge of his comrades. Both 1st and 2nd Battalions saw much service in the South African War, the 2nd Battalion forming part of the garrison which defended Ladysmith for 120 days.

In the war of 1914-18 the regiment consisted of 21 battalions and took part in all the main actions on the Western Front, including Mons, Loos and the battles of Ypres, the Somme and Arras. The 2nd Battalion also served in the Italian campaign of 1917-18.

In the 1939-45 war the Gordons served in France and Belgium, Malaya, North Africa, Sicily, Italy, Burma and North-West Europe.

BATTLE HONOURS:

Mysore, Seringapatam, Egmont-op-Zee, Mandora, Corunna, Fuentes d'Onor, Almaraz, Vittoria, Pyrenees, Nive, Orthes, Peninsula, Waterloo, South Africa 1835, Delhi 1857, Lucknow, Charasiah, Kabul 1879, Kandahar 1880, Afghanistan 1878-80, Tel-el-Kebir, Egypt 1882, 1884, Nile 1884-85, Chitral, Tirah, Defence of Ladysmith, Paardeberg, South Africa 1899-1902.

Mons, Le Cateau, Marne 1914, '18, Ypres 1914, '15, '17, Loos, Somme 1916, '18, Ancre 1916, Arras 1917, '18, Cambrai 1917, '18, Vittorio Veneto.

VICTORIA CROSSES:

Awards of the Victoria Cross since 1914.

Lt. J. A. O. Brooke, 18/2/15, Gheluvelt, Belgium.
Dmr. W. Kenny, 18/2/15, Nr. Ypres, Belgium.
Lt. A. E. Ker, 4/9/19, St. Quentin, France.
Pte. G. McIntosh, 6/9/17, Ypres, Belgium.

REGIMENTAL TARTAN :
  Gordon tartan.   It is worn by all ranks, including the band.

REGIMENTAL MARCH :
  " The Cock o' the North."

REGIMENTAL JOURNAL :
  The Tiger and Sphinx,
    Gordon Barracks,
      Aberdeen.

REGIMENTAL ASSOCIATION :

  The Gordon Highlanders Club,
    25 Crown Street,
      Aberdeen.

  Branches at Aberdeen, Edinburgh, Glasgow, London,
  Perth, Arbroath and Hawick.

AFFILIATED REGIMENTS :

  The London Scottish.

  Canadian
    The 48th Highlanders of Canada.

  Australian
    5th Battalion (The Victorian Scottish Regiment).

  South African
  The Queen's Own Cape Town Highlanders.

THE QUEEN'S OWN
CAMERON HIGHLANDERS
[79th]

THE QUEEN'S OWN CAMERON HIGHLANDERS

THE regiment was founded in 1793 by Alan Cameron of Erracht under a Letter of Service authorising him to raise a Highland regiment. It was numbered the 79th and was first called the Cameronian Volunteers, this name being changed in the following year to 79th Cameron Highlanders. The regimental tartan was designed by Cameron's mother, who was a MacDonell of Keppoch, and is a combination of the Cameron and the MacDonald tartans.

The regiment had scarcely completed its equipment when it was ordered to Flanders to support the armies under the Duke of York against the French. Following that campaign orders were issued for the 79th to be drafted into four other regiments, but after a stormy interview between Cameron and the Duke of York the order was rescinded. The regiment was then sent to Martinique where it suffered so severely from disease and from illegal drafting that on its return to this country it had to be largely re-formed. The first campaign in which the 79th came into personal conflict with the enemy was in 1799 in Holland, where it gained its first battle honour for its share in the attack on Egmont-op-Zee. In 1801 it formed part of Sir Ralph Abercromby's expedition to Egypt and for its services was granted the distinction of the Sphinx superscribed " Egypt."

From 1809 to 1813 the regiment was engaged under the Duke of Wellington in driving the French out of Portugal and Spain. It took part in all the major battles of the Peninsular campaign and specially distinguished itself at Fuentes d'Onor. The 79th was one of four regiments specially mentioned by Wellington in his dispatch on the battle of Quatre Bras. At Waterloo the 79th formed square and withstood the charges of the enemy cavalry whilst the pipers played spirited airs inside the square and one, Piper Mackay, played round the outside. All its senior officers were either killed or wounded and the regiment returned to its bivouac under the command of Lieutenant Alexander Cameron, a nephew of the founder.

The regiment was in the Highland Brigade in the Crimean War and won special praise for its conduct on the Alma and at

Sevastopol. In the Indian Mutiny it was present at the final capture of Lucknow and in the subsequent pursuit captured the colours of the 7th Oude Irregular Infantry and four of the enemy's guns.

In 1873 Queen Victoria directed that the regiment should thenceforth be styled " The Queen's Own " and the facings were changed from green to blue to denote the royal connection. The Thistle, ensigned with the Imperial Crown, was also granted as a badge. When the army was reorganised in 1881 the 79th became the only single battalion regiment and it remained so until a 2nd Battalion was raised in 1897.

At Tel-el-Kebir, in the Egyptian campaign of 1882, Private Donald Cameron was the first man in the brigade to gain the top of the enemy's trenches and at Atbara in 1898 the regiment had the honour of leading the British brigade. In the South African War General Smith-Dorrien said of the Camerons, " You have done more marching than any other regiment in South Africa but I have never met a more uncomplaining regiment."

In the war of 1914-18 the Camerons raised 13 battalions and fought with much distinction on the Western Front and in Mesopotamia and Macedonia. At the battle of Loos, five battalions took a prominent part.

In the 1939-45 war the regiment served in France 1939-40, Burma, Western Desert, Eritrea, Sicily, Italy and North-West Europe.

BATTLE HONOURS :

Egmont-op-Zee, Corunna, Busaco, Fuentes d'Onor, Salamanca, Pyrenees, Nivelle, Nive, Toulouse, Peninsula, Waterloo, Alma, Sevastopol, Lucknow, Tel-el-Kebir, Egypt 1882, Nile 1884-1885, Atbara, Khartoum, South Africa 1900-02.

Marne 1914, '18, Aisne 1914, Ypres 1914, '15, '17, '18, Neuve Chapelle, Loos, Somme 1916, '18, Delville Wood, Arras 1917, '18, Sambre, Macedonia 1915-18.

VICTORIA CROSSES :

Awards of the Victoria Cross since 1914.

T/Lt.-Col. A. F. Douglas Hamilton, 18/11/15, Hill 70, France.

Cpl. J. D. Pollock, 18/11/15, Hohenzollern, France.
Pte. R. Tollerton, 19/4/15, Aisne, France.

REGIMENTAL TARTAN :
79th or Erracht Cameron tartan. It is worn by all battalions and the band.
In 1943 H.M. The King gave permission for the regimental pipers to wear kilts of the Royal Stewart tartan to commemorate the 150th anniversary of the raising of the regiment.

REGIMENTAL MARCHES :
Quick Time .... " Pibroch o' Donuil Dhu "
                           (Pipes and Drums).
Slow Time .... " Logie o' Buchan " (Band).

REGIMENTAL JOURNAL :
The 79th News,
    Cameron Barracks,
        Inverness.

REGIMENTAL ASSOCIATION :
Cameron Barracks,
    Inverness.

Branches — Edinburgh, Glasgow, Dundee, Arbroath, Highland, Fife, London and Sheffield.

AFFILIATED REGIMENTS :
The Liverpool Scottish (T.A.).

Canadian
The Queen's Own Cameron Highlanders of Canada.
The Cameron Highlanders of Ottawa.

Australian
16th Battalion (The Cameron Highlanders of Western Australia).
37th/39th Battalion (The Henty Regiment).
52nd Battalion (The Gippsland Regiment).
61st Battalion (The Queensland Cameron Highlanders).

New Zealand
Ist Battalion Southland Regiment.

F

THE ARGYLL AND SUTHERLAND HIGHLANDERS (PRINCESS LOUISE'S)
[91st-93rd]

THE ARGYLL AND SUTHERLAND HIGHLANDERS

THE regiment as it is now known was formed by the union in 1881 of the 91st (Argyllshire Highlanders) and the 93rd (Sutherland Highlanders). The 91st became the 1st Battalion and the 93rd the 2nd Battalion.

The 91st was raised in 1794 by the Duke of Argyll in response to an appeal from the King when Britain was threatened by the French Republicans.

The 93rd was raised under the patronage of the Sutherland family in 1800 also at a request from the Throne. A proportion of the able-bodied sons of tenants on the Sutherland estates were required to join the ranks of the Sutherland regiment as a test of feudal duty, and this form of conscription is believed to have been the last instance of the exercise of feudal influence on a large scale in the Highlands.

Both regiments went into action for the first time at the Cape of Good Hope, the 91st in 1795 and the 93rd n 1806. The 91st was present at the victories of Roleia and Vimiera in the Peninsular War and gained much credit in the memorable retreat of Sir John Moore on Corunna during which it formed part of the rearguard and was seven times engaged with the enemy. It rejoined Wellington in time to take part in the desperate struggles in the Pyrenees, and fully maintained the best traditions of Scottish valour on the Nivelle and at Nive, Orthes and Toulouse.

In 1814 the 91st was fighting at Bergen-op-Zoom in Holland while the 93rd was engaged at New Orleans. The 93rd lost 520 officers and men in the fruitless attack on the formidable entrenchments at New Orleans.

In the Crimean War the 93rd formed part of the Highland Brigade, which distinguished itself at Alma, Balaclava and Sevastopol. At Balaclava the regiment won immortal fame when, under Sir Colin Campbell, it formed line in two ranks and repelled a charge of Russian cavalry, gaining the title of " The Thin Red Line." The Argylls have the distinction of being the only infantry regiment to bear the honour, "Balaclava."

The outbreak of the Mutiny in 1857 took the 93rd to India where it participated in the storming of the Secundrabagh and the capture of the Shah Nujjif to bring succour to the garrison of Lucknow. Seven officers and men of the 93rd received the Victoria Cross for gallantry during the Mutiny.

The 91st was engaged in the Zululand campaign of 1879, this being the last occasion on which they carried their colours in action.

On the amalgamation in 1881 the new regiment took the title of Princess Louise's (Sutherland and Argyll Highlanders). This was later changed to Princess Louise's (Argyll and Sutherland Highlanders) and subsequently again altered to its present title.

The 1st Battalion embarked for South Africa in October 1899, and joined the forces under Lord Methuen in time to take a prominent share in the battle of Modder River. It later formed part for some time of the famous Highland Brigade, and while with it took part in the memorable night attack on the Boer position at Magersfontein. The 3rd and 4th Battalions (Militia) also served in South Africa.

In the war of 1914-18 the regiment expanded to 27 battalions and served on the Western Front and in Macedonia and Palestine.

In the 1939-45 war it saw much action in France, 1940, Malaya, Abyssinia, Crete, North Africa, Sicily, Italy, and North-West Europe.

The Argylls have the right to march through the Royal Burgh of Stirling with bayonets fixed, flags flying and drums beating.

BATTLE HONOURS :

Cape of Good Hope 1806, Roleia, Vimiera, Corunna, Pyrenees, Nivelle, Nive, Orthes, Toulouse, Peninsula, South Africa 1846-7, 1851-2-3, Alma, Balaclava, Sevastopol, Lucknow, South Africa 1879, Modder River, Paardeberg, South Africa 1899-1902.

Mons, Le Cateau, Marne 1914, '18, Ypres 1915, '17, '18, Loos, Somme 1916, '18, Arras 1917, '18, Cambrai 1917, '18, Doiran 1917, '18, Gaza.

VICTORIA CROSSES :

Awards of the Victoria Cross since 1914.

Lt. W. D. Bissett, 6/1/19, Maing, France.

2nd/Lt. J. C. Buchan, 22/5/18, Marteuille, France.

Lt. J. R. N. Graham, 14/9/17, Mesopotamia.

2nd/Lt. A. Henderson, M.C., 5/7/17, Fontaine-les-Croisilles, France.

Capt. J. A. Liddell, 23/8/15, Ostend-Ghent, Belgium.

T/Lt. D. L. MacIntyre, 26/10/18, Nr. Henin, France (attached H.L.I.).

T/Lt.-Col. L. MacL. Campbell, D.S.O., 2/6/43, Middle East.

Maj. J. T. McK. Anderson, D.S.O., 29/6/43, North Africa.

REGIMENTAL TARTAN :

The 42nd tartan. It is worn by all ranks and by the band and pipers.

The Argylls are the only regiment to wear a plain red and white dicing on the glengarry and feather bonnet.

REGIMENTAL MARCHES :

" The Campbells are Coming."

" Highland Laddie."

REGIMENTAL JOURNAL :

The Thin Red Line,
    The Castle, Stirling.

REGIMENTAL ASSOCIATION :

114 West Campbell Street,
    Glasgow, C.2.

Branches at Glasgow, Edinburgh, Stirling and London.

AFFILIATED REGIMENTS :

Canadian

The Argyll and Sutherland Highlanders of Canada (Princess Louise's) (M.G.).

The Calgary Highlanders.

Australian

41st Battalion (The Byron Regiment).

YEOMANRY AND SCOUTS

THE AYRSHIRE YEOMANRY
(EARL OF CARRICK'S OWN)

THE AYRSHIRE YEOMANRY

THE Ayrshire Yeomanry is the senior yeomanry regiment in Scotland and the seventh yeomanry regiment in Great Britain. It was formed in 1793 by Archibald, Lord Kennedy, being then known as the Ayrshire Yeomanry Cavalry. When, in 1838, there was a general disbandment of yeomanry regiments only two—the Ayrshire and the Lanark-shire—were retained in Scotland.

During the South African War the volunteers from the Ayrshire and Lanarkshire Yeomanries served in the campaign as the 17th Company of the Scottish Battalion of Imperial Yeomanry.

In the war of 1914-18 the regiment was originally on active service in Gallipoli and Egypt. In January, 1917, the Ayr-shire Yeomanry and Lanarkshire Yeomanry were formed into the 12th (Ayr and Lanark Yeomanry) Battalion of the Royal Scots Fusiliers. The division to which the battalion was then attached was composed mainly of yeomanry units and was popularly known as the "Broken Spurs." The battalion took part in operations in Palestine and thereafter served on the Western Front.

In the 1939-45 war the regiment fought as the 151st and 152nd (Ayrshire Yeomanry) Field Regiments, Royal Artillery, in North Africa, Italy and North-West Europe.

The family of the present commanding officer Lieut.-Colonel Hamilton-Campbell, hold the unique honour of having commanded the corps at intervals for four generations in direct line.

The regiment has now been re-formed as a unit of the Royal Armoured Corps.

BATTLE HONOURS :

South Africa 1900-02.

Ypres 1918, France and Flanders 1918, Gallipoli 1915, Rumani, Egypt 1916-17, Gaza, Jerusalem, Tell 'Asur, Palestine 1917-18.

REGIMENTAL MARCH :

" The Garb of Old Gaul."

REGIMENTAL ASSOCIATION :

Ayr.

THE LANARKSHIRE YEOMANRY

THE LANARKSHIRE YEOMANRY

THE first yeomanry in Lanarkshire — the Upper Ward Yeomanry, later the Upper Ward and Airdrie Yeomanry— was raised about 1819. In 1838 many of the yeomanry regiments were disbanded, only two, the Ayrshire and Lanarkshire, being retained in Scotland. In 1852 the regiment was renamed the " Lanarkshire Regiment of Yeomanry Cavalry."

On the outbreak of the South African War a mounted infantry battalion of four companies was organised from the Scottish Yeomanry. The volunteers from the Lanarkshire Yeomanry formed part of the 17th Company of the 6th Battalion of Imperial Yeomanry. The 17th Company arrived in South Africa in March, 1900, and served there until the end of the campaign.

On the reorganisation of the Yeomanry in 1901 the regiment was designated the Lanarkshire Imperial Yeomanry. In 1908 it became part of the Territorial Force and the word ' Imperial " was dropped from the title.

In the war of 1914-18 the regiment served in Gallipoli and Egypt. At the beginning of 1917 the Lanarkshire Yeomanry and Ayrshire Yeomanry were amalgamated to form the 12th (Ayr and Lanark Yeomanry) Battalion of the Royal Scots Fusiliers and after much strenuous work in Palestine, fought on the Western Front until the end of the war. Sergeant Thomas Caldwell was awarded the V.C. for gallantry while in command of a Lewis gun section near Elseghem in October, 1918.

In the 1939-45 war it was originally a yeomanry unit but later was converted into artillery, forming the 155th and 156th Field Regiments. The 155th was badly cut up at Singapore and the 156th served in North Africa, Italy and North-West Europe.

On the reconstitution of the Territorial Army in 1947 the regiment was converted from artillery to armour and is now a unit of the Royal Armoured Corps.

BATTLE HONOURS :

South Africa, 1900-02.

Ypres 1918, France and Flanders 1918, Gallipoli 1915,

Egypt 1916-17, Gaza, Jerusalem, Tell 'Asur, Palestine 1917-18.

REGIMENTAL ASSOCIATION :
  Regimental Headquarters,
    Carluke.

THE LOTHIANS AND
BORDER HORSE YEOMANRY

THE LOTHIANS AND BORDER HORSE YEOMANRY

THE present regiment is the successor of three yeomanry regiments all of which were raised in the year 1797. Two of these, the Berwickshire Yeomanry Cavalry and the Royal Midlothian Yeomanry Cavalry, were disbanded in 1827 and 1871, respectively. Sir Walter Scott was for a time Quartermaster, Paymaster and Secretary of the Royal Edinburgh Volunteer Light Dragoons, later merged in the Royal Midlothian. The third was originally named the East Lothian Yeomanry Cavalry, but in 1888 its title was changed to the Lothians and Berwickshire Yeomanry Cavalry.

In the South African War the Lothians and Berwickshire Yeomanry constituted the 19th Company of the 6th (Scottish) Battalion of Imperial Yeomanry and took part in many engagements during the campaign.

After the South African War the regiment was much increased in size and became the Lothians and Berwickshire Imperial Yeomanry, but on the formation of the Territorial Force in 1908 the title was altered to the Lothians and Border Horse.

In the war of 1914-18 the corps consisted of three squadrons. " B " squadron served on the Western Front, being eventually absorbed into the 17th Royal Scots, while " A " and " D " squadrons served first in France and later in Macedonia.

The regiment was converted in 1921 into the 19th (Lothians and Border Horse) Armoured Car Company, Royal Tank Corps, and in 1936 it became an Armoured Regiment, a second regiment being added in 1939.

In the 1939-45 war the 1st served in France until St. Valery, after which it was re-formed and served in the North-West Europe campaign as a Flail Regiment until the end of the war. The 2nd fought in North Africa and Italy as an Armoured Regiment equipped with Sherman tanks.

The regiment is now a unit of the Royal Armoured Corps, with the full title of The Lothians and Border Horse Yeomanry.

BATTLE HONOURS :
  South Africa 1900-01.

  France and Flanders 1915, Doiran 1918, Macedonia
  1915-18.

REGIMENTAL ASSOCIATION :
  20 Great King Street,
    Edinburgh.

THE QUEEN'S OWN
ROYAL GLASGOW YEOMANRY

THE QUEEN'S OWN ROYAL GLASGOW YEOMANRY

THE Glasgow and Lower Ward of Lanarkshire Yeomanry Cavalry was formed in 1848, replacing the Glasgow Light Horse, which had been in existence from 1796 till 1822. The regiment provided an escort for Queen Victoria when she visited Glasgow in August, 1849, and in token of her approval of the splendid appearance of the corps on that occasion, Her Majesty subsequently conferred on it the honorary distinction of the Queen's Own Royal Regiment.

The corps was on active service in the South African War as part of the 6th (Scottish) Battalion of Imperial Yeomanry.

In the war of 1914-18 the regiment consisted of three squadrons of which " A " and " B " served on the Western Front and " C " in Gallipoli and Palestine.

In 1921 it was converted to Field Artillery, and in 1938 it became the 54th Anti-Tank Regiment, another regiment —the 64th—being added in 1939.

In the 1939-45 war the regiment served in France 1940, in Singapore, the Western Desert, Sicily, Italy and North-West Europe.

It was placed in " suspended animation " in 1946 but on the reconstitution of the Territorial Army in 1947 it was reborn as a unit of the Royal Armoured Corps, bearing the title " The Queen's Own Royal Glasgow Yeomanry," R.A.C. (T.A.).

BATTLE HONOURS :

South Africa 1900-01.

Loos, Ypres 1917, '18, Passchendaele, Somme 1918, Bapaume 1918, Ancre 1918, Courtrai, France and Flanders 1915-18.

REGIMENTAL ASSOCIATIONS :

(*a*) Queen's Own Royal Glasgow Yeomanry Association.

[Open to members who served up to 1921.]

Secretary.—Craigmuir,
Coltpark Avenue,
Bishopbriggs.

(*b*) Queen's Own Royal Glasgow Yeomanry Regimental Association.

[Covering those who joined the regiment after it became Artillery.]

Secretary.—Crimond,
Glasgow Road,
Kirkintilloch.

THE FIFE AND FORFAR YEOMANRY

THE FIFE AND FORFAR YEOMANRY

THE history of yeomanry regiments in both Fife and Forfar dates from the end of the 18th century. The first Forfar regiment was raised in 1794 and the first Fife regiment about 1798. These corps were disbanded and re-formed at various periods. In 1860 the Fifeshire Mounted Rifle Volunteers, later the Fifeshire Light Horse Volunteer Corps, was raised and in 1876 the Forfar Light Horse Volunteer Corps.

On the outbreak of the South African War, volunteers from the Fife and Forfar Light Horse formed part of the 20th Company Imperial Yeomanry. The company embarked for South Africa early in 1900 and during its service in the campaign received in all about 500 officers and men from the Fife and Forfar.

In 1901 the regiment became the Fife and Forfar Imperial Yeomanry. The " Imperial " was dropped from the title on the formation of the Territorial Force in 1908.

In the war of 1914-18 the regiment went into action for the first time at Gallipoli. When the change from mounted to dismounted units took place towards the end of 1916, it became the 14th (Fife and Forfar Yeomanry) Battalion, The Black Watch, and served in Egypt and Palestine 1917-18 and in France 1918.

It was later converted into a unit of the Royal Armoured Corps. On the outbreak of war in 1939 two regiments were formed. One formed part of the British Expeditionary Force in 1939 and both, after D-day, fought in the North-West Europe campaign.

BATTLE HONOURS :

South Africa 1900-01.

Somme 1918, Bapaume 1918, Hindenburg Line, Épéhy, France and Flanders 1918, Gallipoli 1915, Egypt 1915-17, Gaza, Jerusalem, Palestine 1917-18.

REGIMENTAL MARCH :
" Wee Cooper o' Fife."

REGIMENTAL ASSOCIATION :
Cupar.

Local branches at Cupar, Dunfermline, Dundee and Kirkcaldy.

THE LOVAT SCOUTS

THE LOVAT SCOUTS

SOON after the outbreak of the South African War Lord Lovat obtained War Office permission to form a special corps of stalkers and game-keepers used to riding, stalking and shooting in rough mountainous country. The first corps of 250 men, horse and foot, went to South Africa in March 1900 and so marked was its success that Lord Lovat returned to Scotland to recruit more men. In a few days he had 1,000 applications and two new companies of Lovat's Scouts were formed. In a dispatch General Sir Archibald Hunter said of the corps in South Africa : " As scouts, spies, guides, on foot or pony, as individual marksmen or as a collective body in the fighting line, they are a splendid band of Scotsmen which is the highest compliment I can pay them."

In 1903 two regiments of yeomanry, each 500 strong, were formed called the 1st and 2nd Lovat's Scouts, converted later into The Lovat Scouts.

In the war of 1914-18 the corps served in Gallipoli, Egypt and Macedonia and from 1917 onwards as specialised scouts, snipers and observers on the Western Front.

In the 1939-45 war the regiment garrisoned the Faroe Islands from 1940 to 1942, thereafter trained as mountain troops and special ski troops in Canada and served in Italy from May, 1944, until the end of the war.

The corps has now been reduced to squadron strength and amalgamated with the Scottish Horse, Royal Armoured Corps.

BATTLE HONOURS :

South Africa 1900-02.

France and Flanders 1916-18, Macedonia 1916-18, Gallipoli 1915, Egypt 1915-16.

REGIMENTAL TARTAN :

Fraser tartan.

REGIMENTAL MARCH :

" The Lovat Scouts March."

REGIMENTAL ASSOCIATION :

Branches at Inverness, Edinburgh, Glasgow and London.

THE SCOTTISH HORSE

THE SCOTTISH HORSE

THE Scottish Horse is unique in that it was originally raised, not in Scotland, but in South Africa. In 1900 the Caledonian Society of Johannesburg offered to form a corps under the name of the " Scottish Horse " to be recruited from Scotsmen in South Africa. In 1901 a regiment of four squadrons was raised under the command of the Marquis of Tullibardine, afterwards the Duke of Atholl. Later Lord Tullibardine, with the assistance of the Caledonian Society of Melbourne and the Royal Highland Society of London, raised a second regiment, consisting of Scotsmen from home and Australians of Scottish descent.

The two regiments served with much distinction in the South African campaign and Lieutenant W. H. English, of the 2nd, was awarded the V.C. for gallantry at Vlakfontein in July, 1901.

The regiment was disbanded after the South African War but, soon after, Lord Tullibardine raised two regiments in Scotland as units of the Imperial Yeomanry.

On the outbreak of the war of 1914-18 the Scottish Horse was enlarged to a brigade of three regiments with second and third lines, making nine regiments in all. It served as infantry in Gallipoli and Egypt. Subsequently the 1st and 2nd regiments were amalgamated to form the 13th (Scottish Horse) Battalion, The Black Watch, and fought in Macedonia and towards the end of the war on the Western Front.

In 1919 the regiment was again disbanded, but in the following year it was re-formed this time as " Scouts," with a certain proportion of horses. In 1936 it was re-designated " Cavalry " and fully horsed but in 1940 it was mechanised and became the 79th and 80th (Scottish Horse) Medium Regiments, R.A.

In the war of 1939-45 the 79th took part in the landing in Normandy and in the subsequent operations in North-West Europe, while the 80th fought in Sicily and throughout the Italian campaign.

The Scottish Horse is now a unit of the Royal Armoured Corps and affiliated to the 4th/7th Royal Dragoon Guards.

BATTLE HONOURS :

South Africa 1900-02.

Hindenburg Line, St. Quentin Canal, Beaurevoir, Selle, Sambre, France and Flanders 1918, Macedonia 1916-18, Gallipoli 1915, Rumani, Egypt 1915-16.

REGIMENTAL TARTAN :

Murray of Atholl.
The pipers wear the Tullibardine tartan.

REGIMENTAL MARCH :

" The Scottish Horse March " (composed by the Duchess of Atholl).

REGIMENTAL ASSOCIATION :

Glasgow and Aberdeen.

ANGLO-SCOT REGIMENTS

THE LONDON SCOTTISH

THE LONDON SCOTTISH

THE Highland Armed Association of London (or Loyal North Britons) was raised in 1793 as part of the country's volunteer forces, ready to repel Napoleon's threatened invasion of England. This corps was disbanded in 1816 but in 1859, sponsored by the Highland Society of London, and acting in co-operation with the Caledonian Society, a group of influential Scots in London raised the London Scottish Rifle Volunteers under the command of Lord Elcho, later the Earl of Wemyss.

During the South African War the regiment found three service sections which served with the 1st and 2nd Battalions of the Gordon Highlanders and were present at the engagements at Houtnek Poort, Doornkop and the battle of Diamond Hill.

In the war of 1914-18 the 1st Battalion of the London Scottish was the first Territorial Infantry Battalion in action against the Germans—at Messines on Hallowe'en, 31st October, 1914—and it continued to serve in France and Flanders throughout the war. The 2nd Battalion went overseas in 1916 and served in France, the Balkans and Palestine, being present at the capture of Jerusalem on 9th December, 1917.

In the 1939-45 war the 1st Battalion joined the 8th Army in North Africa, took part in the invasion of Sicily and in all the major battles of the Italian campaign, including the Anzio Bridgehead and the breaking of the Gothic Line, and eventually formed part of the Army of Occupation at Trieste. The 3rd Battalion, a Heavy A.A. Unit, after being in action during the Battle of Britain as part of the A.A. Defence of London, fought throughout the Sicilian and Italian campaigns, often in the rôle of field artillery. From the three battalions some 1,400 officers were commissioned to Scottish and other units.

Members of the regiment won two V.C.s in the 1914-18 war and one in the 1939-45 war.

The regiment is affiliated to The Gordon Highlanders.

BATTLE HONOURS :

South Africa 1900-02.

Messines 1914, Ypres 1914, '17, '18, Givenchy 1914, Loos, Somme 1916, '18, Arras 1917, '18, Cambrai 1917, '18, Valenciennes, Doiran 1917, Jerusalem.

REGIMENTAL TARTAN :

Elcho tartan (Hodden Grey).

REGIMENTAL JOURNAL :

London Scottish Regimental Gazette.

REGIMENTAL ASSOCIATION :

Old Comrades' Association,
59 Buckingham Gate,
London, S.W.1.

Branches at Edinburgh, Glasgow and Aberdeen. There are also several overseas branches, including at Sydney, Vancouver, Calcutta, Singapore, Durban and Jerusalem.

ALLIED REGIMENT :

Canadian
The Toronto Scottish Regiment (M.G.).

THE LIVERPOOL SCOTTISH

THE LIVERPOOL SCOTTISH

EARLY in 1900 a petition organised by an influential committee was presented to the War Office requesting permission to raise a volunteer corps of young Scotsmen in Liverpool on similar lines to the London Scottish. Authority was granted on 30th April, 1900, for the formation of a battalion to be called the 8th (Scottish) Volunteer Battalion, The King's Liverpool Regiment.

In response to a call for volunteers to serve in South Africa, a service section was formed and attached to the 1st Battalion, Gordon Highlanders. They arrived too late to take part in any major engagements but did valuable work on detachment in various blockhouses.

On the formation of the Territorial Force in 1908 the regiment became the 10th (Scottish) Battalion, The King's (Liverpool) Regiment.

In the war of 1914-18 two battalions served on the Western Front. The 1st Battalion received special commendation for its conspicuous gallantry on 16th June, 1915, in the attack on Bellewaarde, in which 75 per cent. of the battalion were casualties. Captain Noel G. Chavasse won the V.C. and bar whilst serving as Regimental Medical Officer.

In 1938 the regiment became a battalion of the Camerons with the official title " The Liverpool Scottish, The Queen's Own Cameron Highlanders."

In the 1939-45 war the 1st Battalion was on home service until going out to garrison Gibraltar in December, 1945. The 2nd Battalion was converted in 1942 into the 89th Anti-Tank Regiment, R.A.

In 1947 the 1st Battalion was re-raised as a Motor Battalion in 23rd Independent Armoured Brigade and the 2nd Battalion as 655 L.A.A./Searchlight Regiment, R.A.

BATTLE HONOURS :

South Africa 1902.

Bellewaarde, Somme 1916, Ypres 1917, Pilckem, Menin

Road, Passchendaele, Cambrai 1917, Lys, Estaires, France and Flanders 1914-18.

REGIMENTAL TARTAN :

Forbes tartan.

REGIMENTAL MARCH :

" Glendaruel Highlanders."

REGIMENTAL ASSOCIATION :

7 Fraser Street,
    Liverpool, 3.

THE TYNESIDE SCOTTISH

THE TYNESIDE SCOTTISH

In October 1914 the War Office authorised the formation of a battalion to be raised by the Tyneside Scottish Committee and to be designated " The Tyneside Scottish." Within 28 days a complete Tyneside Scottish Brigade of four battalions was raised and within the next three months two reserve battalions were added. The regiment differed from the London Scottish and the Liverpool Scottish in respect that the latter were recruited mainly from Scots by birth or parentage, whereas the majority of the Tyneside Scottish in the 1914-18 war were Scots by adoption.

The Brigade consisted of the 1st/4th Tyneside Scottish (20th/23rd Battalions Northumberland Fusiliers) and took part in many actions on the Western Front, notably the battles of the Somme 1916 and Arras 1917 and the heavy fighting of March-April 1918. By the end of April 1918, the Brigade as a formation had ceased to exist save a remnant of the 3rd Battalion which was re-formed and returned to France later in the year.

On the expansion of the Territorial Army in 1939 the duplicate battalion of the 9th Durham Light Infantry was authorised to be raised as the 12th D.L.I. Tyneside Scottish, and later was affiliated to The Black Watch. Towards the end of 1939 the unit became known as the 1st Battalion Tyneside Scottish, The Black Watch, and in 1940 took part in operations in France until Dunkirk. Only 140 members of the battalion survived death or capture to make their way across the Channel. After being re-formed the battalion served in Iceland and later took part in the landing in Normandy and subsequent fighting until August, 1944, when the battalion was broken up.

The regiment has now been re-constituted as a Light Anti-Aircraft Regiment and remains affiliated to The Black Watch.

REGIMENTAL TARTAN :

The 42nd (Black Watch) tartan.

REGIMENTAL MARCH :

Same as The Black Watch.

During the 1939-45 war the tune " Donald's awa' to the War " was adopted as a battalion march.

REGIMENTAL ASSOCIATION :

Members of the regiment are eligible for membership of The Black Watch Association.

OTHER SCOTTISH UNITS OF THE
BRITISH COMMONWEALTH

AUSTRALIA

Scottish Units of the Australian Military Forces during the 1939-45 War.

Unit	Service in 1939-45 War	Affiliated to
1. 5th Inf. Batt. (Victorian Scottish Regiment).	Northern Territory.	The Gordon Highlanders.
2. 2/5th Inf. Batt.	Palestine, Libya, Greece, Syria, New Guinea.	
3. 16th Inf. Batt. (The Cameron Highlanders of Western Australia).	Northern Territory, New Britain.	The Queen's Own Cameron Highlanders.
4. 2/16th Inf. Batt.	Matruh, Syria, Tripoli, New Guinea, Borneo, Celebes.	
5. 25th Inf. Batt.	New Guinea, Bougainville.	K.O.S.B.
6. 2/25th Inf. Batt.	Syria, Tripoli, New Guinea.	
7. 27th Inf. Batt. (The South Australian Scottish Regiment).	New Guinea, Bismarck Archipelago, Bougainville.	
8. 2/27th Inf. Batt.	Palestine, Syria, New Guinea, Borneo.	
9. 30th Inf. Batt. (The New South Wales Scottish Regiment).	New Guinea.	The Black Watch
10. 2/30th Inf. Batt.	Singapore, Malaya.	
11. 37th (later 37/52) Inf. Batt. (The Henty Regiment).	New Guinea, New Britain.	The Queen's Own Cameron Highlanders.
12. 41st (later 41/2) Inf. Batt.	New South Wales.	The Argyll and Sutherland Highlanders.
13. 42nd Inf. Batt.	New Guinea, Bougainville.	The Black Watch
14. 61st Inf. Batt. (Queensland Cameron Highlanders).	New Guinea, Bougainville.	The Queen's Own Cameron Highlanders.

Note 1.—Prior to the 1939-45 war Scottish units in Australia wore the same tartans as the Scottish regiments to which they were affiliated.

Note 2.—The 5th Inf. Battalion (Victoria), 16/28th Inf. Battalion (Western Australia) and the 30th Inf. Battalion (New South Wales) are the only Scottish units in the post-war Citizen Military Forces.

CANADA

A. Canadian Scottish Units which served in the war of 1939-45.

Unit	Service in 1939-45 War	Tartan
1. The Black Watch (Royal Highland Regiment) of Canada.	U.K., N.W. Europe.	42nd (Black Watch). Pipers wear the Royal Stewart tartan.
2. The Highland Light Infantry of Canada.	U.K., N.W. Europe.	Mackenzie.
3. The Lorne Scots (Peel, Dufferin and Halton Regiment).	U.K., Italy, N.W. Europe.	Campbell of Argyll.
4. The Stormont, Dundas and Glengarry Highlanders.	U.K., N.W. Europe.	MacDonnell of Glengarry.
5. The North Nova Scotia Highlanders.	U.K., N.W. Europe.	Murray of Athol.
6. The Cape Breton Highlanders.	U.K., Italy, N.W. Europe.	42nd.
7. The Cameron Highlanders of Ottawa (Machine Gun).	U.K., N.W. Europe.	Erracht Cameron
8. The Essex Scottish.	U.K., N.W. Europe.	MacGregor.
9. The 48th Highlanders of Canada.	U.K., Italy, N.W. Europe.	Davidson.
10. The Argyll and Sutherland Highlanders of Canada (Princess Louise's).	U.K., N.W. Europe.	42nd.
11. The Queen's Own Cameron Highlanders of Canada.	U.K., N.W. Europe.	Erracht Cameron
12. The Calgary Highlanders.	U.K., N.W. Europe.	42nd.
13. The Seaforth Highlanders of Canada.	U.K., Italy, N.W. Europe.	Mackenzie.
14. The Canadian Scottish Regiment (Princess Mary's).	U.K., N.W. Europe.	Hunting Stewart.
15. The Toronto Scottish Regiment (M.G.).	U.K., N.W. Europe.	Elcho (London Scottish).

B. Canadian Scottish units now in the Canadian Army Reserve Force.

    (i) (*a*) The regiments at A above.
         (*b*) The New Brunswick Scottish.
            The Pictou Highlanders (Motorised).

    (ii) The following four artillery units formed from Scottish units :

          9th Anti-Tank Regiment (Self Propelled) (Argyll Light Infantry).

          59th Light Anti-Aircraft Regiment (Lanark and Renfrew Scottish).

          66th Light Anti-Aircraft Regiment (Canadian Scottish Regiment).

          54th Light Anti-Aircraft Regiment (Scottish Fusiliers).

Note.—The Irish Regiment of Canada wear a saffron kilt and is believed to be the only Irish regiment in the Commonwealth in which all ranks wear the kilt.

NEW ZEALAND

The New Zealand Scottish.

SERVICE IN 1939-45 WAR :

Both 1st and 2nd Battalions were fully mobilised on the entry of Japan into the war. The 1st Battalion was selected as one of the two Territorial battalions to serve overseas and embarked for New Caledonia in December, 1942, as part of the 15th Brigade, 3rd New Zealand Division. The 15th Brigade was disbanded in July, 1943, and personnel transferred to other units. Most of the members of the battalion subsequently served in the Islands Campaign and later in the Middle East.

TARTAN : The 42nd (Black Watch) tartan.

Note.—The New Zealand Scottish is the youngest Territorial unit of the New Zealand Military Forces. It came into being officially on 17th January, 1939, and was allied in May of that year to The Black Watch. Only persons of proven Scottish birth or descent were eligible for membership. During the war a second Battalion was formed and located in the South Island, the first Battalion in the North Island. In the post-war Territorial Army the regiment has become part of the Armoured Corps as the 1st Divisional Regiment, R.N.Z.A.C. (New Zealand Scottish).

SOUTH AFRICA

Unit and Colonel-in-Chief	Service in 1939-45 War	Tartan	Affiliated to
1. Witwatersrand Rifles H.M. The Queen.	Italy.	Douglas.	The Cameronians (Scottish Rifles).
2. Cape Town Highlanders H.M. The Queen.	Middle East, Italy.	Gordon.	The Gordon Highlanders.
3. Transvaal Scottish H.M. The King.	1st Batt. East Africa, Middle East. 2nd Batt. Middle East. 3rd Batt. East Africa, Middle East.	Murray of Athol and Murray of Tullibardine.	The Black Watch.
4. The First City The Duke of Montrose.	Madagascar, Italy.	Graham.	
5. Pretoria Highlanders.	Madagascar, Nossi Bay Landings.	Hunting Stewart.	

Note 1.—The Cape Town Highlanders (Duke of Connaught and Strathearn's Own) were re-designated " The Queen's Own Cape Town Highlanders " from 1st October, 1948.

Note 2.—The Transvaal Scottish is the only Commonwealth Scottish regiment entitled to two tartans.

Note 3.—All the above regiments form part of the post-war Coast Garrison and Active Citizen Forces of South Africa.

Note 4.—During the war of 1914-18, the South African Scottish regiment was the 4th South African Infantry Battalion. It was recruited from the Scottish regiments in the Union, the 1st and 2nd Transvaal Scottish and the Cape Town Highlanders, and from members of the various Caledonian Societies. The regiment wore the Murray of Athol tartan.

HONG KONG

Scottish Company of the Hong Kong Volunteer Defence Corps.

SERVICE IN 1939-45 WAR :

Mobilised in 1941 and fought with the corps throughout the hostilities in Hong Kong. Their main action was at Stanley, on the island, where they suffered heavy casualties.

After the cease fire on 25th December, 1941, most of the corps were made prisoners of war.

TARTAN : Gordon.

Note.—The Corps was founded in 1854. Their first Hon. Lieut.-Colonel was William Caine, then Attorney General in the Hong Kong Government and formerly an officer in The Cameronians.
Scots by birth or ancestry are eligible for membership of the Scottish company, which is drawn from the business community of the colony and from local government officials.

SHANGHAI

Scottish Company of the Shanghai Volunteer Corps.

The Shanghai Volunteer Corps was formed in 1844 and served periodically in times of civil commotion and external aggression up to 1941. It consisted of about 1,500 men of the following nationalities: British, American, Scandinavian, Russian, Portuguese, Filipino, Chinese and Japanese. When Japan entered the 1939-45 war, she sent troops into Shanghai immediately, disbanded the corps and interned the members of the Scottish Company along with all other British subjects.

TARTAN : Hunting Stewart.

FEDERATED MALAY STATES

Scottish Platoon of the 2nd Selangor Battalion, Federated Malay States Volunteer Force.

TARTAN : Hunting Stewart.

Note.—There were formerly two Scottish platoons in the F.M.S. Volunteer Force, one in the 1st Perak Battalion and the other in the 2nd Selangor Battalion. The Scottish platoon in the Perak Battalion was united with the Batu Gajah European Platoon No. IX about 1937, but the platoon in the Selangor Battalion remained Scottish until the outbreak of war in the Far East in December, 1941, when the Force was called out for active service.

SINGAPORE

Scottish Company of the Singapore Volunteer Corps.

SERVICE IN 1939-45 WAR :

The corps was on active service during the Malayan campaign and was captured by the Japanese on 15th February, 1942.

> *Note.*—The Scottish ("C") Company of the corps was formed in 1922 but was later amalgamated with "A" (M.G.) Company to form "S" (Support) Company of the 1st Battalion. There is at present no Scottish company in the corps.

INDIA

The Calcutta Scottish.

This was a British volunteer unit of the Auxiliary Force, India (A.F.I.) and was composed of Scots by birth or ancestry, drawn mainly from the business community in Calcutta.

The unit was disbanded on 15th August, 1947.